Author's note

The Hunt clan offspring now number about two hundred and are scattered over a wide area of this continent. We have, collectively, visited every corner of Australia yet remain a very connected family. We sometimes don't see each other for years but we are always aware of what is happening to other family members and where they are. We range in age from one to eighty-three years, and there are presently three of us in our eighties.

The nomadic influence of our heredity is strong in all aspects of our lives. While many of the men in our family have worked in a range of bush occupations, seasonal and otherwise, the Hunt women have also married men of a similar nature.

Despite the anguishes, heartbreaks and challenges over the years, we have moved with the times, integrated in society and accepted change, whilst always maintaining the spirit of our Aboriginality and our deep-rooted pride in our origins within this great land.

Harold Hunt

St Mary's, New South Wales, 2006

Memoirs from the Corner Country

The Story of May Hunt

HARLOD HUNT

Memories of Nanna

The most succinct way to describe Nanna is that she was proud of her people, her family, her achievements and herself. Everyone she met, including her opponents, admired her. There was a quiet strength and confidence about her, and a spiritual depth that drew people near.

As a child I liked to believe that I was her favourite. As an adult I came to realise that it was Nanna's way of making everyone feel special.

Nanna was an imposing woman. She was large and dark, with silver hair that fell to her waist, and strong arms that nestled me into her bosom. Her scars bore testament to her physical adventures. A lump in her shoulder at the age of seventy-three came from the continual rebound of a twelve-gauge shotgun, and a .22 calibre bullet rested alongside her spine. Yet she remained the epitome of femininity and strength.

Nanna's laughter still rings, her voice resonant. In the Aboriginal way it was the impression of what she said, not necessarily the words, that made you believe her and love her.

Family came first, a tradition that is still inherent through generations of our family. Her honesty, love and intelligence continue to live through us, her children.

Gail Hunt, youngest daughter of Harold and Nellie Hunt

To the memory of May Hunt and her family.

Forever loved.

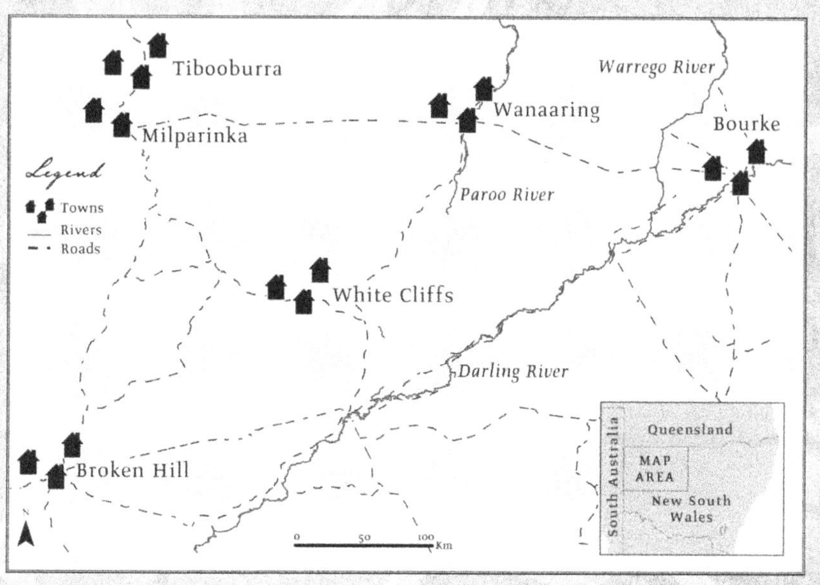
Tibooburra
Milparinka
Wanaaring
Warrego River
Bourke
Legend
Towns
Rivers
Roads
Paroo River
White Cliffs
Darling River
Broken Hill
South Australia
Queensland
MAP AREA
New South Wales
0
50
100
Km
N

One of the early Australian settlers was William Feilden Hamilton. His mother, Frances Eliza Feilden, was the fourth child of Sir William Feilden, First Baronet of Feniscowles, Lancashire, England.

On 2 April 1842, Frances Feilden married Andrew Hamilton, a merchant in Leith, Scotland. She was his third wife and they had seven children before he died in 1853.

William, or Bill as he was known, was born into this aristocratic Scottish family in Streatham, London, in 1849. He had four older sisters and two younger sisters. Bill was only four when his father died and he was unable to recall any memory of him. His mother, it was said, had little love for her son or boys in general, and was seen as a strict and harsh mother.

When he was old enough Bill was sent to school at Haileybury, but he became ill and was later sent to a tutor in Switzerland. For the next three years he did little other than to learn French fluently.

At the age of seventeen his mother sent him to Australia, paying £300 a year for him to be a cadet on a sheep station.

Bill found himself working on a station in the Corner Country in western New South Wales. He was an ambitious young man and it took him only a year to realise that he was doing all the hard work, while his employers were the ones being paid. He soon left and took up sheep droving.

Later Bill partnered up with Emil Geyer, who owned stores in Wentworth and Wilcannia, and together they took 250,000 acres of land in Malyangapa country between Yancannia and Wonnaminta. Emil became known as the 'remittance man' – putting up Bill's share of the money for the property. Located about forty miles west of the little opal mining town of White Cliffs, the property was originally known as Mordent Station but later had its name changed to Morden.

Emil continued to operate his businesses, while Bill was left to run the station.

Malyangapa country sits in a small area of the Corner Country. It extends from Milparinka to Lake Frome and its surrounds, to the head of Yancannia Creek in the east as well as to Mt Arrowsmith and then south to Mootwingee and Sturt Meadows. The Malyangapa people and their boundaries overlap other language groups, namely the Bandjigali, Wadigali and the Wiljali.

The Malyangapa people led a semi-nomadic life and moved through their country in seasonal cycles. They ate meats such as kangaroos, lizards, goannas, birds, emus and bandicoots, complemented by plants and seeds. Waterholes, soaks and springs were important as the country was dry and prone to drought. The waterholes were all named and well cared for.

The Malyangapa had no contact with white people until explorer Charles Sturt arrived in 1846. They were content to observe him and his adventurers, as they had already heard tales of strangers travelling through the area and not settling.

However, the pastoralists who followed in Sturt's footsteps did settle and they introduced the sheep and cattle that would devastate the countryside and destroy the delicate relationship that the Malyangapa had held with the land for thousands of years.

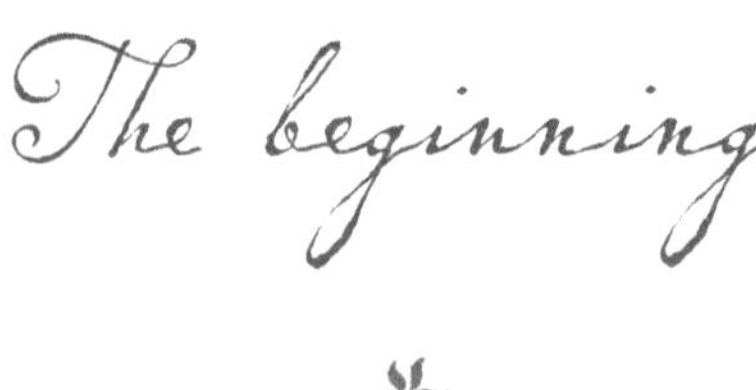

The beginning

Bill Hamilton began his new life on Mordent Station. He built his homestead beside a substantial waterhole which was topped up by a run-off from the gently sloping hills in the west.

Bill went to great lengths to manage his property – he talked with the remaining elderly Malyangapa stockmen who worked on neighbouring properties and learned from them. These stockmen were the traditional owners of the land that Mordent was on and they knew the country well. They spoke to Bill about the seasons and the fall of the land as well as about the stories that made up their country and the significance of certain areas to the men and the women. The old stockmen helped Bill understand Malyangapa country.

One day when Bill was out checking his property, his horse stumbled and fell, throwing him off and leaving him miles from home with a broken pelvis. He had no water and no means of communication. Although he knew his horse would eventually go home and be seen, there would be no way of knowing which direction it came from unless the horse was noticed arriving. There were many tracks around the homestead and yard from the constant flow of traffic.

It was a grim situation as Bill was exposed to the glare from the sun and heat off the land. He was at the mercy of marauding dingoes, pesky crows and ants, and the bush's ability to exaggerate the most ethereal noises increased his anxiety. The hours dragged by and Bill, hoarse from shouting, strained for sounds that might signal help was at hand.

Drifting in and out of consciousness, he was finally awakened by a noise and he sensed a presence close by. Afraid to open his eyes, Bill held his breath and listened for a clue that would identify who or what his company was. Soon he was able to make out the language of the Malyangapa. He lay quietly as he didn't know who they were or what their intentions might be.

The clattering of spears and boomerangs onto the stony earth was followed by the sound of feet padding towards him. Bill opened his eyes to the harshness of the sun and to faces he was unsure he wanted to see. He looked at the strangers and saw kindness.

The Malyangapa men spoke softly to each other, and water was produced in a possum-skinned bag and slowly administered to Bill. Eventually he was able to understand that they were going to carry him back to the homestead. He was lifted up, draped across the men's shoulders and carried home over the rugged terrain.

At dusk back at the homestead, a rider set out for White Cliffs with a spare horse to bring out the local doctor. It was late before the doctor departed town with his bag of instruments and chloroform. While riding in the darkness the doctor's horse stumbled and fell, breaking the bottle of chloroform and making the resetting of Bill's pelvis an even more painful operation.

During his period of incapacitation, Bill's staff of cook, housekeeper and stockmen catered for his needs. His gratitude was conveyed to his rescuers and not long after he got well he took a Malyangapa wife and named her Fanny.

Fanny's traditional name was only used when she was in the company of her own people. Her totem, the bony bream fish, could be found in the slow-moving rivers and waterholes around that area. The bream was considered a delicacy among her people.

Soon the unlikely couple celebrated the birth of their only child, Hannah. The young girl grew up learning the ways of both Aboriginal and European culture. She complemented her traditional skills, such as weaving reeds and string from the bark of certain trees into baskets and bags, with the European art of embroidery, knitting and crocheting. She learnt about European eating habits and was shown how to bake bread and cook stews and desserts on a fuel stove. Hannah also spent her time learning other domestic pursuits, such as mending clothes and washing and ironing.

Although Hannah never lived traditionally, she was not denied the pleasure of attending corroborees or playing with her Aboriginal brothers and sisters. As she grew older, pastoralist women like the squatters' wives and governesses working on nearby stations took an interest in her and continued to teach her the many domestic jobs they had spent their own lives perfecting. Hannah was a quick and keen learner who was supported and encouraged by her family.

Although Bill knew his family was settled, he had plans to move on. It was his intention to take Fanny and Hannah back with him to England for a time and then return with them and settle in New Zealand. He truly believed his family and friends would accept his wife and daughter.

Bill's plans had never been acceptable to Fanny. The distant lands made it clear that it meant leaving her people forever. She knew that her husband would take great care of her and Hannah, but it would mean being disconnected from her family, her community and her spiritual values and associations. Her traditional country was her lifeblood and what she knew. All that she had been taught and valued was tied to the earth. Bill was an honest and kind man but his plans sparked fear in her heart. Fanny had seen many children being taken away by drovers, graziers and the government and most were never heard of again.

Bill was used to Fanny going away on hunting excursions or attending ceremonies. Her absences were never frowned upon or worried about. However, soon after discussing the move, Fanny went away with Hannah and Bill knew there was a difference. He realised that Fanny and his daughter were never coming back.

Bill saddled his horse and for two weeks he rode over the countryside, his feelings fluctuating between hope and despair. With no luck locating his family, Bill approached one of the elders who told him why the union had ended and why they wouldn't be found. Fanny had chosen a life that she understood. The news devastated him.

Earlier, in 1882, after Bill had successfully established Mordent and the breeding of its sheep, he had been offered £60,000 - a sum he refused at the time. Now, after three years of drought and the disintegration of his family, Bill walked off without a penny and Emil Geyer's investment was lost.

Back to country

Fanny took Hannah back to her people and it was not long before Fanny married a young man named Cobham Tommy Williams. Hannah quickly settled into her new life and because she had enough skill in English she was able to share her knowledge with the other children.

In the early days of settlement, it was an unspoken rule that Aboriginal people be given the name of their employer, usually with the name of the station added. 'Cobliam Tommy' was derived from Tommy growing up and working on Cobliam Station – a neighbour to the Hamilton property – for a man named Williams. It was not unusual to meet brothers with different surnames. This did not interfere with their traditional names or obligations – it just kept the boss man happy.

A child was soon born to Tommy and Fanny, a little boy christened Gilbert but known to all as Dinjo. With two children and a husband to care for, Fanny spent her time in the camp, going on hunting trips and caring for her children. She left the jobs of cooking and house work to the younger, single girls whom she had trained during her days as Bill Hamilton's wife.

Both Tommy and Fanny could see that the European culture and lifestyle was going to have a big effect on their lives and that their children had to be informed. This was not too difficult. Tommy and Fanny had long been exposed to the language and habits of the Europeans. Their children were comfortable in both worlds and were in demand as station staff – Hannah as cook and house-maid, and Dinjo as stockman. As they became adults these skills enabled them to move around the countryside.

Dinjo was a forward-thinking young man who took advantage of opportunities. He was fully initiated into traditional Aboriginal law and he had a strong spiritual grounding.

One of the attractions for young Aboriginal men during this time was the enticement to go to war. World War One had begun and Dinjo, along with a few of his mates, was impressed by the uniforms and the stories being told by the men who had enlisted. It all sounded exciting – not only was there a trip overseas but there were adventures they had never dreamt about. So Dinjo enlisted into the armed services.

It was soon discovered that he was a 'full-blood' as well as being an initiated man. In those days full-bloods could not be accepted into the armed services and Dinjo was discharged. It was a huge blow. He had already commenced training in the Light Horse Brigade so that he could work with horses, and he had looked resplendent in his uniform.

However, Dinjo did not give up and made inquiries about other services. He was soon accepted into the South Australian police force as a tracker. All went well until he tracked down a criminal who turned out to be a member of that service. That incident cost Dinjo his job and was a tough moment in his young life. He felt he could not win.

Dinjo made the decision to return to the life of a stockman and bush worker, which meant that he was with family and back in a lifestyle he'd known from childhood.

It was the hand of fate that brought Hannah Hamilton's future husband into her life. Like Hannah, Jack Quayle had a white father and an Aboriginal mother. He took a contract to break in a number of horses on the station where Hannah was working and they saw each other on a daily basis. Jack usually went to the workers' dining room for his meals – a privilege not available to the 'station blacks', as the initiated men were referred to. After a while, it seemed natural they would marry.

Hannah sought the permission of her family and elders before going ahead with the wedding, and it was with their support that she married Jack Quayle in a little church in the village of Milparinka, twenty-five miles south of the township of Tibooburra. The union was seen by all to be the beginning of a happy life.

Milparinka sits on the south-eastern fringe of the Simpson Desert on a stony ridge above a mile-long waterhole. It lies between the rocky outcrops and gibber plains of the west and the softer brown loam and red sandhill country of the east. This lake country is traditional Malyangapa country. Small creeks and the mighty Bulla River top up the lakes to maintain a permanent water supply.

The young couple were in demand throughout the Corner Country. While Jack enjoyed the travelling and the lifestyle, he also planned for the future. He saw the need for more water throughout the area as many pastoralists and settlers were taking up land, and they relied on the government to provide watering places along the stock routes. Waterholes along major creeks often dried up during dry periods, leaving a critical situation for both stock and drovers. Jack's knowledge in finding water and sinking dams guaranteed him long-term contract work and he took Hannah along to cook for the men he employed. Between the dam-sinking contracts Jack continued horse breaking, which enabled him to indulge in his love of horses. He had the security of never being unemployed.

Some dams were usually nothing more than sizeable waterholes ranging in depth from ten to fifteen feet and a hundred yards square at ground level, depending on how often they were de-silted. The catchment areas of the dams were drains constructed several hundred yards across the sloping terrain.

When there was a quick downpour of rain, the water would be channelled into a smaller catchment area known as a silt tank. Here, most of the topsoil being washed along the drains would settle before the water level reached a height where it would overflow into the main dam.

Jack's father, Jack Quayle Senior, had been a dam-sinker in the Corner Country. Like many European men at the time, he took himself an Aboriginal partner, although he never considered her as his wife or equal. This attitude was not unusual. Three sons were born in quick succession, Jack Junior, Jim and Bill, and by the time the boys had reached late adolescence their parents had separated.

The boys' mother had returned to her family, leaving them to be raised by their father. She had been unhappy living with Jack Sr. Not only did he not respect her, but she had found it difficult to adjust to his culture and understand its ways.

Jack Sr made all the decisions and everything had to be done the way that he liked. Eventually, she felt she had no other choice but to leave her boys and hope that when they were adults they might understand her decision and try to re-establish a relationship with her.

Jack Sr had total influence over his sons and he was their main role model. In those days, many considered looking after 'mixed-descent' children as a bold and heroic deed. They lived in the heartland of their people, yet the boys were not allowed to play with their Aboriginal cousins or to run freely through the bush. They were raised to avoid corroborees and social gatherings and to fear initiation, although they did learn some traditional cooking methods, such as using coals in the ground. The boys could not resist the urge to cook that way, especially when they caught goannas, porcupines or some other delicacy. There were many occasions when their father would tell them not to cook in the 'blackfella way'. Jack Sr told his boys they had to stick to their own kind – 'half-castes' – and he even barred them from mixing with his own associates.

May's father, big Jack Quayle –
about 20 years of age.

There were times, though, when, without their father's knowledge, they would go away on short hunting expeditions with some of the younger men of their mother's family, who often called by the Quayle camp and workplace.

Despite their father's dominance, the young men did not consider themselves white, although they were careful to avoid the possibility of being initiated. Their father had instilled great fear in them about that. However, young Jack Jr had instincts and ideas his father never suspected. When the old man was not around, he told his brothers to remember what their mother had told them. Jack Jr knew there were some things they must never forget.

The boys worked with their father until his death at the Tibooburra hospital. Later, they found out through the traditional grapevine that their mother had also died.

Jack Quayle Sr, without an official will, saw fit to leave his dam-sinking plant to his sons. However, this was not to be. The station manager at Olive Downs, where they had all been working at the time of their father's death, claimed that Jack Quayle had been in debt to the station. The manager withheld the plant – several scoops, ploughs, horses and their harness, along with camping equipment such as camp ovens, tents and water drums. The boys were left with nothing other than the skills that their father had passed on and their valuable experience as stockmen and bushmen.

Jack had already made up his mind that he would do contract work and that he would be the employer. His skills were many and his determination to succeed limitless. He set out and continued to do earthmoving jobs on other stations by using their equipment until he was able to acquire some of his own. This didn't take long. He also excelled as a horse breaker and there was plenty of that kind of work in the Corner Country as horses were used in all forms of transport. Jack felt that his future was secure.

Mid-summer was hot and dry, and surface water was scarce. The waterholes away from the river and the smaller dams would not always see out the season. Special care had to be taken when travelling with horse-drawn vehicles to ensure water was available at the dams in twenty to thirty-mile intervals. Some water was carried for domestic use but there had to be water at night and morning for the horses. Even when good grass was nearby and nutritious, it was often dry and the horses would wander in search of water.

Reliable information from people and contractors passing through was sought by graziers and pastoralists to find out if there was a need to move away from the rivers and instead travel between watering places, such as artesian and subartesian bores and the larger government-owned dams. These were usually well managed as they provided water for travelling stock being brought in by drovers to railheads or abattoirs in the bigger towns and cities.

This situation restricted the number of sheep and cattle that graziers were able to manage and there was an obvious need for someone with expertise in finding water and dam-sinking.

The couple went on to raise a large family. The first of their fourteen children was born in a bush camp. There was a hospital in the small town of Tibooburra but the Quayles' work kept them in a fifty to one-hundred-mile radius of the town. Not that distance really mattered as Aboriginal women were not hospitalised for childbirth. Of the children born to Jack and Hannah, only eight survived to adulthood.

Following the birth of Ruby, their second daughter May was born in Milparinka on 1 May 1900.

The family decided to settle in Tibooburra where there was a doctor and a chance that the children might be accepted into the local school. At the time of the Quayles' arrival in town, the number of white students was fewer than that required to maintain a teacher, so eventually some 'half-castes' were enrolled. The fact that Jack had been raised in the district and was well-known and respected made the family's adjustment to town life much easier.

Marjory was born soon after their arrival in Tibooburra, followed by Jack, Laurie, Monica, Frank and Edith. The children adjusted to the discipline of school and they enjoyed having playmates. The girls were conscientious and were taught cooking and domestic camp-keeping by their mother while the boys followed in their father's footsteps.

By 1912, mechanisation had arrived in the back blocks – motor vehicles ushered in a new era. It was all very exciting for the boys who were mechanically minded. Unlike horses, there was no need to find food and water for the motor vehicles at the end of each day. This was definitely something different.

There was one child among this family who was unusual, and that was May. With a ready smile as her trademark, May was a fun-loving, confident teen. She was a little daring, always on the go, always doing the unexpected, and would often be found hunting with a pack of kangaroo dogs that were her constant companions.

May yearned to belong to both sides of her world – the male and female – and the advent of the motorcar reduced the competition from her brothers in regards to the relationship with her father and horses. They were the two greatest loves in her life. Being with her father and her horses made May's world complete.

She loved the solitude of the bush and her work, like horse-tailing, allowed her to lose herself in it. Horse-tailing required May to go into the scrub in the early hours of the morning and round up horses. She would bring them into the yards where her father would select the ones he needed for handling. It was during this time that May developed exceptional skills in riding and in general horse handling. She was a natural.

Jack Quayle had the greatest confidence in his daughter. May's carefree response to the concern her parents showed when she went kangaroo hunting alone was, 'What do you think Mum? You think old man kangaroo will get me or something?' And sure enough, one day he did.

May was out rounding up the horses to be brought in for handling. She and her company of dogs were wandering through the bush, noting tracks and keeping a sharp ear for the slightest sound of a horse bell. Suddenly a 'big red', or buck kangaroo, was disturbed from its rest in the shade. With Big Red's late night and early morning feeding time over, it was time for siesta. The scent of the approaching dogs reached him and the kangaroo made his move – the chase was on.

Owing to his size and confused state of drowsiness, the excited dogs had him surrounded in no time. Big Red did what all big old bucks do in such a situation – he stopped and turned to fight.

Rising high on powerful legs and leaning back on his sturdy tail, Big Red stood his ground. As each dog came within reach, he inflicted sufficient cuts and scratches with his razorsharp claws to keep the dogs from closing in. Although the dogs were only able to make contact when his attention was drawn by another attack, they were unrelenting.

The fight continued for some time with Big Red standing firm and soon the dogs began to tire. One of the exhausted dogs moved in and fastened his teeth into Big Red's thigh. The dog was unable to let go and move away before it found itself in a deadly grip. Holding the dog tightly to his chest and biting it savagely, Big Red tried to get his feet up and into contact with his attacker. It had reached crisis point.

With one of her dogs about to be disembowelled, May knew she had to intervene. She grabbed a tree branch and struck the kangaroo with a heavy blow to the back of his head. The blow only served to attract the kangaroo's attention. He let go of the dog and pulled May into a death lock and began to bite her around the head and shoulders.

Instinctively, she reached up and gouged his eyes with her thumbs. The eye gouging lessened the ferocity of the attack, but the situation spurred the dogs into a frenzied assault. Big Red was forced to surrender May and attempted to flee. He was exhausted, which enabled the dogs to bring him down.

The battle ended with May and her dogs bloodied and shaken but all in one piece. Undaunted, she went back to her task, which was to round up the horses. Her major concern was what she would tell her mother when she got home. How could she defend her argument that she was always safe on her own? If it hadn't been for the dogs, she knew the roo would probably have killed her.

May decided to talk to her dad first, guessing that he would understand. On her arrival back at camp, she avoided going for breakfast and fronting her mother. Then came a call from the camp proper.

'May, what you doin' muckin' around? Come and get your breakfast. Is somethin' wrong?'

'No Mum, nothin' wrong.'

'Well, what you go and change your shirt for? Come here girl. Somethin' happened to you out there today. I know when you been in trouble. You're too much of a tomboy, and you too game. You think you can't get hurt. I wish your father would slow you down a bit. I been tellin' you. You gonna get hurt bad one day, I'm gonna talk to him. Look, you tell your father I want him.'

'Please, Mum,' said May, 'I was just galloping through the scrub and a bush caught me, I didn't duck down low enough, that's all.'

'You come here girl. You can't put that over on me.'

As if on cue, Jack Quayle appeared.

'Hey Dad,' May called. 'Mum wants to talk to you.'

Jack spoke first.

'Hannah, that girl, I'm goin' to get down on her. She takes too many risks. She's not frightened of anything. I'll talk to her and make sure she is more careful when she is out with the horses. Now, what do you want me for?'

Hannah knew there was no point in pursuing the matter. Jack was a jump ahead of her. May had gone straight to her father when she arrived home and told him the whole story. Hannah bathed May's wounds with cotton wool and tincture of iodine, which May considered more painful than her injuries.

May at her favourite pastime –
in the saddle.

Sitting beside her father on the horse-yard rails, May received comforting advice.

'May, I trust you. I know you've got common sense but you have to understand that your mother worries about you. Spend more time with her so that she can get to know you, like I know you. Mum will be alright when she knows you don't go doin' things without thinking.'

May took stock of what her father told her and realised that she didn't have to change her attitudes or way of life. All she had to do was restrain her excitement and enthusiasm in her mother's presence. May carried out her share of domestic chores around the camp with an easy flow. They were just preparation and licence to get out and do the real things that made life worthwhile – being outside in the free atmosphere of nature's architecture.

Horse work meant catching and taming horses as well as breaking some of the stouter ones into harnesses. These horses would then pull the various types of vehicles. The smaller, lighter horses would be handled and taught to pull sulkies and light buggies, while the heavier ones were used as riding hacks. Others would be harnessed to heavier vehicles, such as wagons and earth-moving equipment like scoops and ploughs, which were used in the construction of dams, drains and levee banks.

May was strong of stature and was developing into a beautiful woman. Her elegance and beauty came from within, and she was no ordinary person. Her achievements and endurance, her will to 'never say die', and her ability to mature and still maintain gentleness and understanding were just some of the characteristics that were to make this courageous, unstoppable woman a legend in her own lifetime.

With her feet planted in both camps, May's understanding of her Malyangapa ancestry sat easily alongside the challenge of learning the white man's ways. Early in life, May had become aware that the little schooling she did have would be necessary if she was to cope with whatever life had in store for her. Her training in horsemanship would also serve her well in earning a living – riding and driving horses when the necessity arose – as well as hunting kangaroo and emu with the strength of a man to feed her large family. It was these strengths that her father had done his best to nurture.

Some time after May's nineteenth birthday, a young Australian-born Irishman by the name of Bill Hunt found his way into the Quayle gang. Bill was a healthy, energetic, happy-go-lucky type of bloke who settled quickly into the camp life of the Quayles.

Bill spoke little of his family and he neither received mail nor did he write to anyone. However, he did occasionally talk about his parents. He mentioned that they owned a piggery in the small outback Victorian town of Coghills Creek and that his brother, Tom, was a schoolteacher.

Bill was about five foot eight inches and solid. He was broad-shouldered and agile. Bill was an easy mixer and was able to join with the Quayle boys in their athletic activities like running, high jump and long jump as well as boxing. Soon romance blossomed.

Three weeks after May's twenty-first birthday in 1921, May and Bill's wedding took place in the little opal mining town of White Cliffs.

Willangie Station

Bill was offered and accepted a position on Willangie Station some sixty miles north of the thriving metropolis of Broken Hill. It seemed a good opportunity to settle down to a regular job and support his new wife.

Bill's job was as a handyman, maintenance worker and camel driver. The camel team on the station was used to transport wool to the railhead at Tarrawingee, which was some fifteen miles from Willangie. The team also brought back supplies for the station on the return journey.

Bill and May moved out to the station and set up camp. Their first real home was a tent pitched under a stand of leafy ghost gums, which encircled the small stock-watering dam. The tall gums provided shade for Bill and May for most of the day. Gums on the eastern side provided early morning shade, as did the trees on the western rim in the late afternoon. Water was carried in buckets hooked to a wooden yoke carried across the shoulders and Bill would always fill the buckets before going to work each day. On wash days it was up to May to carry whatever extra she might need.

ABOVE *Bill Hunt driving bullocks, Bill Gilby with scoop from Jack Quayle's dam-sinking plant.*
BELOW *Bill Hunt with the tail of a big buck kangaroo.*

All the cooking was done in camp ovens and over an open fire. They had neither fuel stove nor anything that remotely resembled a refrigerator. Fresh mutton was obtained daily from the station homestead and because of the heat had to be cooked on the same day, then kept in a hessian-covered cooler known as a Coolgardie safe.

The Coolgardie safe consisted of a wooden base attached and hung by wires from a shallow water-filled, open-topped container. Strands of hessian acted as syphons to allow the water to gradually seep over and down the sides of the safe, cooling the contents with the help of any breeze.

The safe cooler was usually hung from the ridge pole of the tent, where it would get the breeze and have the benefit of shade from surrounding trees.

Ford and fencing

There was a lot of fencing to be done on Willangie so Bill decided to do some of the work on contract as a means of getting ahead. After a short time, the Hunts were able to buy themselves their first motor vehicle – a T-model Ford utility. As soon as it arrived at the station, Bill took one look at it and said, 'That's not for me. I'll stick to the camels, thanks! My wife will be the one to handle that machine.'

May saw this as a challenge. She took the car for a short test run under the guidance of the salesman, who had brought it out from Broken Hill. May immediately accepted the offer to drive the salesman to Tarrawingee to enable him to catch the train back home.

With her instructor beside her, and Bill and the kids in the back, May took the controls and began the round trip to Tarrawingee railway station. Bill was pleased. May had proved herself and it relieved him of the need to learn to drive, although much later he did learn to reverse the vehicle.

Having the car, which was christened Lizzy, allowed May to go out with Bill on fencing jobs where she was able to help by

The Hunts' campsite at Willangie, tent on right.

running the wire. This meant setting the one-hundredweight coils of wire onto a type of spinning jenny – like an early spinning machine with more than one spindle. May would pull the wire out by hand and thread it through the bored holes in the posts. This was a difficult task as each strain was two hundred yards, making the wire pretty heavy by the time she was pulling the full length. It was especially so if some of the post holes were not in a straight line with the rest of the fence. For each strain this action had to be repeated several times, depending on whether it was a five or six-wire fence.

May's first pregnancy did not disrupt her work or camp life. It was usual for pregnant women in the bush to carry on with their duties. However, when the baby was due it was decided May would go to Broken Hill hospital, some sixty miles away. A couple of weeks before the expected birth date, May was taken by the station owner to Broken Hill where she stayed with the Zada family. The Hunt family had become friends with Khan Zada, an Afghan teamster, many years before.

Sadly, happiness with their firstborn eluded them. Tragedy struck and their little baby boy, Bill, died when he was three weeks old. Before long, two more healthy children were born at the Broken Hill hospital. Roy was born in 1923, followed eighteen months later by Doreen.

The Paroo

Bill had adjusted well to life in the bush and to the Aboriginal-style cooking and eating habits of his family. May and Bill often supplemented their food by hunting and eating bush tucker. There was no shortage of kangaroos, emus, goannas and witchetty grubs, or fruit and vegetables such as quandongs, moley apples, wild spinach, pigweed and yams. The bush tucker list was endless and it made for a different and enjoyable change from the usual spuds, onions, cabbage and carrots.

The little family battled on like that for some time before they decided to make a move and visit May's family. Bill joined his father-in-law, big Jack Quayle, on a fencing job on the Paroo River, about a hundred and sixty miles north-west of Bourke.

May was pregnant again and Bill decided that he would take his wife, his mother-in-law, Hannah Quayle, the smaller children, Roy and Doreen, and May's younger sister Edith to Bourke for the birth of their next child.

The journey

This time May was to enter a private nursing home in Bourke under the management of a midwife. The birth of a child does not always come at the most convenient time and summer in most parts of Australia is hot. May's calculations told her that the baby would be due in the height of summer, when the dry westerly winds blew off the Simpson Desert.

A decision had to be made about which way to traverse the one hundred and sixty mile trip to Bourke. Bill still had no interest in learning to drive the car so their mode of transport was to be a horse-drawn wagonette.

It was decided that the best and safest route would be via Yantabulla and Fords Bridge, which were two small towns on the road to Bourke, near the border town of Hungerford. This wasn't the most direct way but it meant there were watering places for them and the horses, and they would be able to top up their food supplies.

The small towns had general stores, which catered for the basic needs in the bush and they were an important part of the trip, especially to buy biscuits, canned fish or lollies for the children. There was also the telephone service, which was important as May was in an advanced state of pregnancy. She did not consider that she was taking any great risk in leaving the trip to town until late; however, there was always the chance of the unexpected.

The day arrived and the group was ready. The family was to break into two groups. Big Jack Quayle, his sons and daughter Monica would stay behind to keep the camp running. The wagonette was loaded with the adults and children, camping gear, clothes, food and water. The horses were fresh and keen to move out. They wanted to be off but Bill's experienced hands, steady on the reins, kept them to a walk until they became used to the feel of the harness. Everyone settled into their seats as they adjusted to the movement of the wagonette.

Bill travelled as late as possible, but allowed enough time for the women to arrange the bedding and camp before nightfall. He saw to the tired horses, took them to water and then found the sweetest grass he could.

When the evening meal was over, there was quiet time around the fire. The beds were ready to be slept in, the washing-up done and the harness checked for signs of wear. The dust-impregnated grease was wiped from the axles and wheel hubs, and fresh grease was applied in readiness for the next day's journey.

It was always an enjoyable experience to sit around the fire at night, listening to its crackling, popping and hissing, and to watch the flames settle before fading to embers and ash. The fresh night air was full of smells from the earth and trees. Clicking beetles and curious lizards checked upon their new arrivals, and a lone owl softly hooted.

The breaking of dawn was welcomed by birdcalls. The campfire flickered to life as Bill stoked it, making himself a pannikin of tea and rolling a cigarette. After his mug of tea and a smoke, Bill brought the horses into camp and began hitching on the wagons.

Travelling through the bush was never boring. The arid inland had sandhills, rolling plains, stony ridges, black channels and plains, and red, eroded gullies, which carried water from the scalded claypans. The claypans edged sandhills that bordered rich herb-growing watercourses, and it was these areas that provided the more nutritious plant life in times of drought.

Towards the end of the day the little town of Yantabulla emerged from the hopbush scrub. The heat seemed to be dancing off the unpainted corrugated roofs of the hotel, post office, general store and the houses occupied by drovers and road workers. There was a harshness about the town.

On the southern side there was hopbush and turpentine scrub covering the sandhills, which seemed to be keeping watch over a huge box swamp at the rear of the hotel. It seemed that the only thing separating the swamp from the scalded stony ridges that stretched for miles north was the town itself and the main road leading to the border town of Hungerford.

A night's camp at Yantabulla Bore, a mile from the town, enabled the dusty travellers to avail themselves of unlimited water and have a refreshing wash at the side of the black square government-built tank.

Two more days of travelling brought them to the township of Fords Bridge, which was situated on the Warrego River and only two days from Bourke. Fords Bridge was similar in size to Yantabulla but was a much softer-looking place. It was embraced by low scrub and sat in comfort on the slow, muddy waters of the Warrego.

The journey from Fords Bridge to Bourke was relaxed and the countryside had fewer stony ridges and more permanent watering places due to it being more settled. The night was spent beside Kelly's Camp Bore, an artesian bore oozing thousands of gallons of water into a small lake which provided a haven for an assortment of bird life. Kangaroos and emus, together with domesticated animals such as sheep, cattle and horses, joined swans, egrets, water hens, ducks and brolgas.

As exciting as the journey had been, the family were beginning to tire and it was only the excitement of the great river and the big town that was keeping spirits up. The next day they entered the treeless Walkdens Plain and could see a dancing mirage far into the distance. There was nothing to break the monotony of being able to look for mile after endless mile and see nothing. After several hours they came to the edge of the plain and a small rise in

The house in Moore Street, Bourke, where Harold Hunt was born.

the terrain into scrubland. There were patches of turpentine, and small mulga trees entwined among eucalypts and box trees that signalled the overflow from the river proper.

Bill guided the horses onto a level piece of ground in the shade of the box trees that lined a dry billabong, a hundred or so yards from the main channel of the mighty Darling – the big river at last and a night's rest ahead. Being close to the river the night sounds were different to those in the scrublands – the creaking of the gums, whose black bulging buds revealed them to be hundreds of years old, the screeching of possums, and the call of the mopoke bird cut across the otherwise silent night.

Morning broke with a new energy. There was just the last short stretch of the journey over the bridge and a mere five miles into town. The family hoped to find a livery stable to have the horses rested and fed, and then they would locate the doctor's place.

On their arrival, they were directed to a rambling weatherboard house in Moore Street. The house was located on a bend in the river and was run by a respected midwife. Bill was only going to stay a couple of days to see the family settled and give the horses a well-earned rest before he left to make the return journey. The load would be lighter and he would travel back in longer stages to the Paroo.

May's eighteen-year-old brother, Laurie, would drive to Bourke in the Ford and bring the family home.

It was a group of wide-eyed children, speechless with excitement, who spent the next few days taking in the sights of Bourke. They looked in shop windows, sat in cafes enjoying lemonade and ice cream, and stood in the streets enthralled by the people bustling by. There were horse-drawn sulkies, spring carts, drays and buggies and every now and then a car would drive along and park in the street. The kids had seen all of these things in the bush but in the bustling town of Bourke, there were just too many on the move, all the time.

One day they all went up to the railway station and saw the train arrive. It hissed and puffed and clanged and screeched. There was white steam rushing out from underneath the front engine and black smoke coming out of the top. If Uncle Laurie had been there, said the children, he would have fixed it because their car, Lizzy, didn't rattle and clang and blow smoke like the train did – and Laurie was always fixing that.

May knew that the time had come. She was ready to walk down and admit herself into the nursing home. Her mother, Hannah, and the kids accompanied her on the short walk and stayed with her until it was time for tea to be served. Soon after, the little family left to allow May to settle down and rest.

The next morning, the band of country kids chattered, giggled and manoeuvred Hannah up the road to where they hoped the new baby was. They rushed to open the gate and ran up the path.

The children tiptoed through the main door and into the room where May was lying. May smiled and told the children that the new baby had arrived. The children peered over and saw a tiny baby boy.

I, the third son of May and Bill Quayle, was born on the 27th of December 1925 and was named Harold John Hunt.

Bill was having lunch with Jack Quayle and his sons, sitting in the shade of a huge coolabah when a horseman approached. It was the station manager. He handed Bill the telegram and shook his hand. 'May and seven-and-a-half pound baby boy both well. Will be ready to come home at the end of the week. Laurie can come and get us. Love May.'

There were slaps on the back and handshakes all round. Laurie was especially happy. This was his opportunity to drive Lizzy into Bourke all by himself.

The night before Laurie was to leave, Bill gave him directions to find the big weatherboard house. Laurie hardly slept that night and was up and away before sunrise the next morning. He didn't know exactly how long the trip would take but he knew he was going to enjoy every minute and every mile.

It was mostly horse and camel-drawn vehicles that used the unmade roads and tracks, and motor vehicles were rarely seen in this part of the country. Many graziers were still using horse and buggy transport to travel to smaller towns, such as Wanaaring, Hungerford and Yantabulla, and using mail coach if they wanted to do a quick trip to Bourke.

The trip to Bourke was a slow and hazardous one. Laurie had to go over creeks and gullies, and stony ridges covered in grey mulga scrub. Shifting sand built up in places with its drift sometimes obstructed by fallen trees. There was an abundance of wildlife, such as kangaroos, emus, wild turkeys and camels. There were also sleepy, shingle-backed blue-tongue lizards that Laurie swerved to miss. Startled goannas ran up the nearest tree to escape the noisy car. Snakes slithered for cover and slow-moving echidnas rolled into balls.

Laurie was feverish with excitement when he eventually crossed the twelve-mile stretch of black soil and rose up into the wooded sandhills bordering the overflows of the magnificent Darling River. There appeared before him a few houses scattered along the road, a hotel and, towering behind, the bridge with its huge forty-foot windlass that lifted the middle to allow traffic to pass beneath. Could this be Bourke? Laurie then remembered that he had to cross the bridge and continue for another four or five miles.

He began to look out for the beginning of the town proper, so that he would not miss the turn to where May was staying. Soon small numbers of motor vehicles appeared. He had never driven in a town. His driving experience so far had been in the bush, where there was only one vehicle moving at any given time – and it was usually him.

Laurie could see the town of Bourke unfolding. There were houses backed by more houses and as he got nearer he could see that they were all laid out in neat squares and rows. There were straight streets and cross streets. He didn't see any buildings that might have been hotels or shops but he decided that he would look for those tomorrow. All Laurie wanted to do was find the big weatherboard house on Moore Street. He managed to navigate the busy streets of Bourke and eventually found the street that he was searching for.

Homewards

Before long, it was time to leave. The kids were ready and this pleased May no end. She had already had a run-in with the matron – May had reported her to the doctor for not changing the baby often enough. Preparations had been made with the Catholic priest to have the baby christened the day after discharge, and on my first day out I officially became Harold John Hunt.

It was time to return to the camp on the Paroo and back to life with the family. The family went to bed early that night, in preparation for the ride home that would only take one day.

When breakfast was over, Laurie packed all the blankets, clothes and tucker box into the back of Lizzy and was bombarded by the constant flow of instructions coming from his mother and May.

May did her best to help but she needed to keep a close eye on me as I was passed from hand to hand. Packing the utility, or buckboard as it was called in those days, was an easy task. It had raised sides within the width of the wheels, then seating along the sides over the wheels, where the children could sit with their feet on the floor and hold onto the side railing along the backrest.

The important thing was to place the groceries where the kids wouldn't be resting or climbing over them and bursting bags of dried fruit, custard powder and tea. There was also newly baked bread from the baker, meat and sausages from the butcher and fruit. It was a real treat to take fresh food into the bush, only possible thanks to the car. Blankets were carefully wrapped around those goods which would dry out if left uncovered, particularly at that time of the year.

The men at the camp were not sure when to expect the family but three days after Laurie had left, it was clear it would be soon. Towards dusk every day, Bill would look up the track expecting to see a little cloud of dust. Then late one afternoon it was there. It seemed everyone at the camp saw it at the same time, stopped what they were doing and waited.

May was especially relieved to have arrived back safely. The jolting of the Ford and the hot January winds meant that the trip had been especially trying. May smiled, as she was glad to see her father and husband. She told them about the tucker she had received while in care and about her argument with the matron. They all knew better than to say anything.

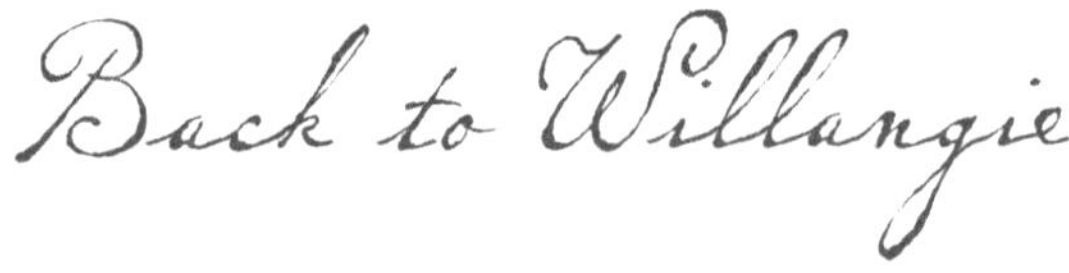

Work with Jack on the Paroo finished once the fencing job was completed. May and Bill decided to return to Willangie. There was still some work there for Bill to complete and Laurie had agreed to go back with them. As well as being able to do all the driving, he wanted to step out on his own. He enjoyed the company of his sister and brother-in-law and he knew that he would always get work with his father on fencing jobs that he had under way.

All went well back at Willangie. Laurie was able to help build a more secure camp in the form of a solidly constructed kitchen-cum-dining room, storeroom and the old standby – a bough shed and a couple of tents. They made a sledge that was cut from a fork in a tree and had decking put onto it, which could be used to cart water in a one hundred-gallon tank to their new home about a half mile from the dam on a clear piece of land.

At that time there was plenty of work for Laurie and Bill. Over the next three years, two more children were born. Beulah and Eric were both born in Broken Hill and again May stayed with the Zada family for the birth of Beulah. May was transported to town in Lizzy a few days before the birth and as soon as she was finished, she would be home and carrying on as usual. When the next baby, Eric, was due we went and camped on a hill on the edge of North Broken Hill, which at the time was referred to as the 'Camel Camp' as there were several Afghan families living there.

Tragedy occurred when a sudden illness took the life of Ruby, May's eldest sister, and left her husband, George, with three young daughters. May being the next in line, she took the eldest, five-year-old Myrtle, while the younger girls, Ada and Mary, went to her parents Jack and Hannah. Myrtle soon became another member of the Hunt family.

Life at Willangie went on. It held a simple freedom as well as an income to feed and clothe the family. While May and Bill didn't have much schooling, they had great foresight as to the need for it. Roy, Doreen and Myrtle began correspondence schooling. The lessons were posted out to the parents to teach. Although May had only grade three primary education, she carried out the task of teaching us with dedication and patience. Schooling at home meant being close to the family. The only other children we could play with were the station owner's children, who were about the same age.

Hunting

Life on Willangie had been good and Laurie being there made things that much better. Though May was capable of driving the Ford, Laurie did most of it, especially when the family went hunting.

A twelve-gauge shotgun and a .22 calibre rifle was standard equipment for hunting trips. A tucker box was usually packed, water bags and a drum filled, and chaff bags thrown on the floor in the back complete with a couple of kangaroo dogs.

They would set out early in the day when the wildlife were feeding and easy to see from a distance, although driving Lizzy often gave the kangaroos and emus early warning. Once the animals were on the move it became the job of the dogs to run them down. With the smaller roos the dogs would do the killing but the big bucks would bail up and fight, which meant there were times when the dogs were badly wounded.

While the adults liked to shoot whatever was available, the children preferred the thrill of the chase. Watching the dogs jump from the back of the vehicle, race in and out among the stumps

LEFT *Harold and sister Beulah.*

RIGHT *Hunt children – Roy, Harold and Doreen.*

and bushes, then fly over abandoned logs was breathtaking. The children couldn't get enough of seeing the dogs in action. Laurie and May would shout out to hang on tight, while Lizzy followed in hot pursuit. At the end of the chase everyone preferred to see the dogs bail up a big roo instead of a smaller one. The box brownie camera was always on hand for blurred photos to be taken in the excitement.

May was very skilled with both the shotgun and the rifle, and she always emphasised the safety aspects of using firearms and the importance of never carrying a loaded weapon. However, on one hunting trip, a member of the family did leave a bullet in the firing position of the rifle he was holding in the back of the wagonette.

Crossing a small steep gully, the jolt of the hard-springed wagonette caused the rifle to discharge. Fortunately the bullet passed through the back rest of the buggy seat before it entered May's back, miraculously missing bone and nerves. The bullet was never retrieved and May was never known to complain, other than to continue to expound the need for safety.

The swaggies

Another favourite pastime for us Hunt children was to go out and meet swaggies. There were numerous names given to the many men who trudged the roads of the outback with their swags during the Depression years. These travellers walked the roads of the Corner Country living off the earnings from an occasional job or from gifts of money or food, and they never seemed to settle anywhere. The swaggies appeared on the horizon slowly emerging from the hazy mirage. They aroused an inexplicable curiosity in me, a wondering – where from and where to?

Whenever a swaggy would come by, I would leave whatever I was doing and drift over into his path. The swaggies seemed old of course, there was a mystery about them. I was always cautious but never scared. We had a German collie, Janet, who would position herself between me and the swaggies, which made every one of our meetings negotiable.

Winter or summer, their attire was the same. A hat, long-sleeved shirt, vest, or waistcoat as it was known then, an old suitcoat which rarely matched the trousers and, of course, solid footwear. Their worldly possessions consisted of a swag, which was always carried in a long thin roll and was about the width of a single bed blanket. It was usually draped over the shoulder, its weight distributed evenly over front and back. Over the other shoulder would be two tuckerbags. Sometimes, there would be a frying pan or small saucepan dangling from the tuckerbags. This left both hands free to carry the most vital utensils of all, a water bag and billycan.

The swagmen would normally just call at the bore, fill their waterbags and, after a short spell, walk to the shade of the large gum trees lining the banks of the nearby creek. Some would rest for a day or so. Others would simply move on.

Only once did one of them come to the house and act strangely. It was an incident I never forgot and it occurred after we had moved to Coally Bore. The swaggy dropped his swag at the corner of the yard, unrolled it and took out his razor and strop. He attached the strop, a flexible piece of leather, to the netting of the fence and began sharpening the blade. Holding the razor he steadily walked to our front gate and stood in silence, just staring. After some time, he returned to his swag and sat with his back against the cornerpost of the yard, not far from our front door.

This behaviour prompted May to pick up one of her firearms. She advised us to stay well inside the house and to be very quiet. She placed herself in the doorway of one of the bedrooms leading off the hall. The swagman again walked to the gate, stood awhile, and then without a word returned to his swag. He bent over and rolled it up without a backwards glance towards the house. He picked up his belongings, threw everything over his shoulders and wandered towards the main road. We watched him go in silence and to our relief he never came back.

On the move

Apart from the swaggies, as children we were not really aware that the Great Depression of the 1930s had set in. It first hit us when the owner of Willangie, Tom Smith, told Bill that he could no longer afford to employ him. It was a bleak time for Tom, too. He was a very fair man and, after discussing the situation with May, Bill talked to his boss. 'Tom, you said if you could help me in any way you would, right?'

'That's right Bill. What have you got in mind?'

'Just a couple of camels Tom, that's all. Those camels you have here are only going to be wandering all over the place until you can afford to pay someone to work them. By then, who knows?'

Bill went on, 'There are two I like and they are already working as a pair in a wagonette, how about them? And those horses of ours, if we can leave two of them here for a while, we can do some travelling and pick up a bit of work, you know, lamb-marking, crutching or a bit of maintenance around some of the bigger stations out on the South Australian side.'

Tom nodded in agreement, 'That's fine with me Bill, you know

Hunt family – Roy, Mum, Beulah, Dad nursing Eric, Harold, Doreen in front.

the camels you want, you just go and take them. Your two horses will be here until you are ready to come and get them.'

The time had come for life to change and we became like gypsies. That suited us kids alright, a new playground every day, going to places we had never heard about. It was an exciting time for us kids but a grim one for our parents. They had to call on all the faith they could muster. With camels yoked to the wagonette and a saddle horse which our parents took turns at riding, we travelled the Corner Country in search of work.

The buggy had two goats tethered to the back axle and a few fowls in a coop. At night the fowls would roost in nearby trees. Janet would help catch them next morning to place them back in the coop for another day's travel. The goats were tethered on long leashes at night so there was fresh milk every day.

With six children on board there was not a lot of room for food and bedding. I remember sleeping head to tail in one bed, which was made up of blankets and bags spread on the ground. Where it was hard, leafy branches were laid down. However, there would often be a sandy creek bed to sleep in.

One such occasion, after a hot day's travel and a good meal of grilled kangaroo and johnnycakes, us kids played in the sand, climbed the big old ghost gums and were happy to be camped in a soft creek bed. All was well until lightning and the deep rumble of thunder awakened May and Bill. A storm had built up in the hills above the campsite. It was a heavy cloudburst and we were awakened by the roar of rushing water, which left no doubt in our minds as to the urgency of the situation.

'There's a flood coming down,' May yelled. 'Can you hear it roar? Quick, everyone get up!' We were all soon in the back of the wagonette, parked a few yards from the top of the bank. We huddled together in the back of the buggy, squirming and wriggling into comfortable positions to wait until daylight. By the time the rain arrived we were under cover with the canvas tent fly unfolded to cover the whole wagonette. It was uncomfortable but dry. By sunrise the storm had moved on. For the adults, it was a relief from the dust, the heat and flies. However, once the excitement was over, it was back to normal.

Bill was not able to get employment for any lengthy period but often got a few days work lamb-marking or crutching at sheep stations. Although this provided some money, he was often paid in flour, tea and sugar or with a tin of jam or treacle.

Mount Browne

Our travels eventually took us back to May's place of birth, Milparinka. There was gold in the hills so we moved out onto Mount Browne Station with the hope that we might get lucky.

May and Bill would spend their days looking for specks of gold, which sometimes could be found lying on the surface of creek beds after flooding. The wind would also expose minute pieces that had to be picked up by wetting a finger and gently touching it to avoid burying it in the soft sand.

We were always told not to venture too far from the camp for fear of becoming lost. We heeded those warnings and found things to keep ourselves occupied. Our main interest was also fossicking for gold, so we played in and around the diggings where earlier prospectors had worked with their dry-blower machines.

These were machines built on wheelbarrows. The dirt would be shovelled onto a metal tray with graded finger-sized holes to allow certain-sized pieces of stone to fall through onto another tray below with smaller holes. This tedious process eventually exposed any gold that might be among the finer particles of sand. The idea was to keep moving the blower from place to place where dirt could be easily shovelled onto it, always leaving behind little mounds of dirt now considered to be without gold. Those mounds suited us kids. We used a similar processing system to the original but our method was more refined. We put small nail holes in shallow tins that had once contained herrings and tomato sauce.

The tins were perfect for sifting though the discarded mounds and we often got exciting results – so exciting we had to show someone. The nearest adult was an elderly prospector camped in the remains of an abandoned stone hut. The old bloke was pleasant and seemed happy to see us when we arrived with our few little specks of gold. He would carefully remove the specks from our fish tins and transfer them to a tobacco tin he kept inside his coat pocket. We would be praised, thanked and told to run off and play like the good little children that we were.

By the time May and Bill arrived back at camp tired and weary, our excitement had waned and they were not told of our findings. One day the inevitable question came.

'What are those fish tins with holes in them for?

'Oh, we just sieve the dirt at those leftover hills where you said other people were looking for gold.'

'And did you find any?' May sternly asked.

We nodded.

'Where is it now?'

'We gave it all to that old man over in that hut. He said it's all right to give it to him.'

May's face was an absolute picture as she looked across to Bill. His mouth was set in a grim line and I was sure he was trying not to laugh.

'Well from now on, don't you go near that old man. Let him find his own gold. We walk all day looking and you kids are giving the stuff away. Just keep it away from him, understand?'

By now another baby was due so the family moved from Mount Browne Station to the outskirts of Tibooburra. May and Bill were adamant that they wanted us to get some schooling.

May couldn't get a house in town as she was Aboriginal and we weren't allowed to camp with the other Aboriginal people on the reserve because Bill was white. It was against the law for white men to live on Aboriginal reserves or in Aboriginal designated areas, or to be in a relationship with an Aboriginal person. So we had to camp a short distance away, which was alright until a new problem surfaced. The government was removing mixed-race kids from their families and placing them into 'care'. May and Bill were not going to be a part of that.

The short stay in Tibooburra had, however, served its purpose as it was a safe place to bring the new baby, Rachel, into the world and a place to catch up with acquaintances.

Bill acquired the lease of a public watering place called Coally Bore, two hundred-odd miles north of Broken Hill and thirty-six miles south of Tibooburra. The bore was only eleven miles away from Milparinka, which now had a pub, a post office and a few houses. On the fringe of the Simpson Desert, it was part of the state's most western stock route, catering for sheep and cattle being driven down from the big holdings further out.

The Coally lease consisted of 640 acres, pastured mainly with stubble and saltbush – not much land on which to graze three horses, two of which Bill had made time to go and fetch from Willangie, and two camels. It suited us when they strayed onto better pastures from time to time.

Coally Bore could be seen as an isolated, lonely place but the nearest neighbours were friendly and offered support whenever we were in need. They were four and five miles away respectively on either side and there were occasional travellers passing by. Some passed in cars or on horse-drawn vehicles and the Afghan teamsters with their camel-drawn wagons moved through, taking supplies to outlying stations.

The Afghans were essential for opening up the vast arid inland areas of Australia. With their camels they were able to traverse huge sandy desert areas, impassable to the hard-hoofed horses and bullocks. It was quite a sight to see an Afghan camel teamster coming in and we were always pleased to see them. We had a lot to do with the Afghans over the years, people like Khan Zada and his family.

Hunting party at Coally Bore.

Bill in white shirt on buggy, May third from right on horseback.

We quickly set up residence in the form of two tents – a brush shelter and cooking galley. In the time that it takes any government department to move, a house arrived from the now defunct town of Tarrawingee, which was a few miles from Broken Hill. It was dismantled in sections and loaded onto a huge horse-drawn wagon. The excitement was overwhelming as we watched the sections being placed together to form the house that we were actually going to live in.

We had never lived in a house before. We had only ever lived in tents and bough sheds. May and Bill would have a room of their own and us boys and girls were to have separate rooms, which meant no longer sleeping in the one big bed. It was also a better place to look after the new baby, Teddy. Teddy was the eighth child and was born at the Tibooburra hospital a short time after the house arrived.

It wasn't long before May tracked down some wild goats and turned them into milk and meat providers. Pigs appeared from god knows where and a garden was soon established. The garden yielded healthy supplements to our diet of damper and brownies, fresh kangaroo, emu, goanna and rabbit meat, and occasional 'wild' sheep.

The going was tough during the Depression and to add to the already hard times, Bill was now stricken with sandy blight or trachoma. When blindness threatened he went to Sydney for treatment.

Bad news

So many new and good things started to happen once our presence at Coally was known. Our grandparents, Jack and Hannah Quayle, and a few other relations came and visited, then moved on to Tibooburra. We all went as far as Milparinka with them and camped beside a big waterhole below the town for a couple of days. For us kids it was a holiday. I recall climbing trees and jumping in and out of the waterhole without the knowledge of the adults.

One day after Jack and Hannah had returned to White Cliffs, the tide turned. May looked out one day and called us over to look at a messenger of bad tidings. She pointed to a small bird, a light blue crane, which belonged to the wetlands but its presence here was an omen.

A few days later, a traveller called in with a telegram from the Milparinka post office. Even before opening it, May knew something was wrong. She clasped the corner of her apron and wiped tears from her eyes. She didn't want to open the telegram.

She went inside and sat on the floor, and we followed and sat touching her. We all began to sniff and wipe our eyes. It was painful to watch May so frightened. Instinctively we knew it had to do with the bird, and we huddled around, leaning on May's lap, kneeling next to her, our arms thrown over her neck and shoulders. With trembling hands, May removed the message from within the black-bordered envelope. None of us could see the few words but we knew that someone had died.

May caved in and sobbed. Her body heaved, 'Oh, my God! My poor dear father has passed away. And I didn't even know he was sick. What will we do without him around any more?' It came out of the blue like a bolt of lightning. Our grandfather, Jack Quayle, had died.

It was the only time I would ever see my mother so broken. Her father, who was everything to her, was gone. That day a big part of May died.

Mum and Granny Quayle at the Coally Bore house,
Harold on the right.

That bird

It happened again. One day while playing alone I saw the same messenger but was not willing to tell anyone. I just wanted it to go away. I wanted someone else to notice it first. I knew the little bird had a message to deliver and I was relieved when May saw it.

We wondered when the bad news was going to come and the family kept looking in the direction of Milparinka. With every cloud of dust, we expected someone to call in with another black-bordered envelope. Later that evening, Bill arrived home from a visit to Yantara Station, some twenty miles east where he went in the hope of getting some work. While out, he telephoned Milparinka to find out if there were any messages and, sure enough, there was a telegram from Marge, May's sister.

Bill went and collected the telegram and brought it back home. It told us that Marge's five-year-old daughter, Hannah, had drowned in the dam at the back of their place. Hannah and her brother had been chasing a rabbit and when it ran down by the water, Hannah followed and slipped into the dam. She was unable to swim and by the time her brother was able to summon help, it was too late.

Grieving was usually shared with other close relations but on these two occasions it was just our family. The separation from the rest of our relatives was painful. There was no phone and no way of seeing anyone without days of travel – for which we had no means, as the faithful old wagonette was in need of repair. They were sad times at Coally Bore for our family.

The goats provided the next incident which was to test May's mettle. Normally, they would go out to graze each morning and return at sundown. One day they didn't return. Instinct, from years of experience, told May that it was not their intention to do so. This was serious. She had to get them back.

The goats were our main source of nourishment, the providers of milk and meat, especially on those occasions when hunting wild tucker was fruitless. We knew we could rely on the goats. There was always a young wether that had been prepared for the dinner table from an early age.

Bill was away in Sydney having his trachoma treated so after giving instructions to Myrtle on how to care for the younger children, May loaded food and a swag onto a packhorse, mounted a riding hack and rode away.

At thirty-two years old, May did not lack determination and courage. She set off to track the goats over stony ridges, sandhills and creek beds. At the end of each day, when the light faded May would unpack her saddlebags, light a fire and tether the horses to graze during the night. She would boil the billy, enjoy a mug of fresh tea, undo the tucker pack and make some johnnycakes to be cooked on the coals. From then on it was fresh johnnycakes and dry salted meat.

May would rise early and breakfast on the cold leftovers. What was left would be rolled in a tea towel and placed in her ration bag. She would begin while the tracks were clear and fresh and the signs indicated approximately how far ahead the goats were.

She knew the goats would make for the shelter of the mighty Koonenberry Ranges from where they originated. She tracked those goats all the way until they reached the ranges, which was home to hundreds of them. There the trail was lost and May finally conceded, life had to go on.

On her return she told us how, on those lonely nights, she would think of her family sitting down to their evening meal and it helped her to go on.

Life at Coally Bore was full and every day seemed to provide something or someone new or different. We enjoyed what we had. May had such a love of horses and riding that she would often saddle up and visit one of the neighbours. It was a break from the family and her time to do a little socialising with her landowner friends. May never allowed race to be a barrier to friendship.

One day May went to visit the Smith family, some five miles away, riding A.B., her big strong bay horse. Somehow he lost his footing and stumbled and fell. May fell heavily onto her left shoulder and broke her collarbone. She remounted and rode home.

Bill was still getting his trachoma treated and May's pain convinced her that she had to go to Tibooburra to see the doctor. She packed some things for herself and Teddy as he was still very young. May had to wait until someone was driving past to get into town. She knew that we would be alright as there was plenty of tucker at home.

It was not long before we saw a cloud of dust and it was heading in the right direction. Beulah and I ran as fast as we could to the main road just in time to wave down the Tibooburra-bound motorist.

'G'day, excuse me mister, our mum's horse fell with her and her shoulder is very sore and it might be broke. She wants to know if you can take her to Tibooburra if you are goin' that far, so she can see the doctor. Mum's got a little baby, too. So she'll have to take him with her, he's too little to leave with us kids. They are ready to go now, if you can give them a lift to the doctor please.'

The driver smiled and nodded. 'Yes, of course,' he said. 'I'll give your mother a lift to the doctor. Hop on the running board and hang on, I'll give you a ride home.' It was only about two hundred yards but the opportunity to have a ride on the running board of a touring car was something not to be missed – even in an emergency.

The car pulled in and it wasn't long before May and Teddy were on their way. She spent a few days in Tibooburra hospital waiting for some swelling to subside before the doctor could reset the fracture and strap her shoulder. He familiarised May with applying and adjusting the sling, which she had to wear for several weeks. Once everything was in order she had to wait for mail day to get a lift home. Not all of this was a bad time. It gave May some precious time with Roy, her eldest, who had been hospitalised earlier with rheumatic fever. Finally, mail day came and May and Teddy made it back to Coally on board a five-tonne wool truck, over bumpy unmade roads.

Shortly after Bill returned from Sydney, the twelve-year marriage ended. I was eight years old at the time. May and Bill had survived hardship and happiness, but all the marriage was doing now was producing more children. May was feeling increasingly isolated from her family and Bill's prolonged absences took their toll.

In Sydney, Bill had his eyes treated at Lidcombe State Hospital and this meant he was forced to stay indoors during daylight and keep away from artificial light at night. He had virtually become a prisoner in his own home and for a strong and capable man this was a big blow.

Once they came to a decision, May called in her brother Laurie. Having packed only a few belongings, we set off to White Cliffs to be with Granny Hannah Quayle. Although White Cliffs was only about 105 miles away, it took more than twelve hours on the unmade roads.

May knew we would be devastated at not seeing our father again – even occasionally was going to be difficult. She told us that he was a good man and was going to be alright. She explained that they could no longer live together and that he might have to stay in Sydney and get treatment for his eyes. We had to move on and stay close to our grandparents and other family, and go to school and learn to read and write. May pointed out that once we learnt that, we could always write to Bill until we saw him again.

I did not fully understand the separation and not having any say in it, I was fearful for the future.

The pain Bill felt that day would have been indescribable. He stood and watched his family drive away in a slow-moving old truck that wound its way across the treeless plains, leaving clouds of dust in the air and a vast emptiness inside his heart.

After leaving Bill and shortly before our arrival in White Cliffs, Roy had a relapse of rheumatic fever and was taken to Wilcannia hospital, sixty miles away. He was not well when the journey began and got worse as the hot and tiring trip progressed. There were tyre blowouts, which made the journey even longer than expected, even with a good run.

Roy became so ill that an emergency midnight call had to be made to the bush nurse at White Cliffs from a station some twenty miles away. The nurse called on the local mail contractor, who was the only available person with reliable transport and the willingness to help out in such circumstances. He came out, put Roy in the dicky-seat of the little single-seater car and headed for Wilcannia and medical care.

Roy had struggled with his illness for more than a year. It was crippling, and not only did his leg joints swell, but it also affected his heart muscles. It could kill him. He had already spent several weeks in Tibooburra hospital and was recuperating when the big move occurred.

However, leaving Coally Bore could not be blamed entirely for Roy's relapse. He was meant to take life easy with no running or other strenuous activities but he had been feeling so well that he neglected to abide by the doctor's orders. Without May's knowledge, Roy had taken on the task of teaching me how to ride a bike and this type of coaching required him to run beside the 'potential champion'. I was devastated when he was rushed away again. Our whole world was falling apart.

White Cliffs

A few miles out from White Cliffs, the land flattened into gibber-covered plains with brown ironstone gravel that led up to white quartz hills, from which the town got its name. I was amazed at the countless mounds of white clay taken from the hand-dug mine shafts covering the stony hills. It was a sight that I couldn't imagine in my wildest dreams, and I was fascinated by this new world. In a basin formed by the surrounding hills was the township.

Two main streets formed a triangle that marked the centre of the town. On one corner was the general store with wide verandahs. Diagonally across was the hotel, the baker and butcher shops, and several houses spreading towards the police station at the eastern end of town.

Opposite was an ugly winding gully that led out past the cemetery. There was another main street that ran north and was bordered by the community hall, church and bush nurse's residence. At the end of this road was the post office and the school. From there on it became another road leading to the most

Hunt and Riley families at White Cliffs.
Aunty Marge Riley standing, May seated holding Teddy.

concentrated part of the diggings, known as the 'open cut'. This was owned and worked by a corporate body employing staff on wages.

Our arrival at the main Aboriginal camps at the top end of town was exciting. There were so many of our relations there to meet us. The last time we were there, our grandfather Jack Quayle and cousin Hannah were present but now they were gone. It seemed that we hadn't really missed them until now. Along with the tears of joy, there were tears of sadness – we had lost so much.

Granny Hannah mentioned to May there was an old tin shack at the bottom end of camp, near her sister Marge's place. Nobody knew who owned it or built it but it was vacant. May promised to fix it up and it wasn't long before we all settled into our new home at White Cliffs.

To supplement the dole, May did laundry work around town and, with the help of her younger brother and sister, sold wood to the townspeople for ten bob a drayload. The three of them, after getting the children off to school, would harness a horse, put together some lunch and, along with a couple of axes and crowbars, head off over the glaring ridges of white quartz.

On a good day it was possible to bring in two drayloads of wood but usually, due to the distance travelled, one load or ten bobs worth was all they got. Even though this was the earnings for two families, it was still a big help as it bought a few loaves of bread, a pound of butter, a couple of tins of jam and a pound of tea. It was much needed money, especially for kids with healthy appetites.

Teddy, the youngest, was the most beautiful, round-faced, chubby bundle of joy. With big brown eyes shaded by locks of black curly hair, he was forever on the move. He loved to play and follow us around – he was our world.

One day our bonny one year old didn't want to play. All Teddy could manage was a tired smile. He'd suddenly become ill. His spirit was strong but his body lost all its strength. Gastroenteritis struck and after a short period, Teddy died. This dreadful virus had taken hold before arrangements could be made to transport him to a doctor.

During this time the second youngest, Rachel, also fell ill and she was taken off to Wilcannia hospital where she spent the next two weeks. May was not able to visit or even talk to her by telephone. It was a very cruel time.

We were all worried about whether we would ever see Rachel again, and May explained that as God had taken care of baby Teddy, the hospital staff would take care of Rachel as they had Roy. May had the responsibility to care for us and to keep us from suffering.

The following days were grim. Adhering to the traditional sunrise and sunset grieving for Teddy, May was joined by family

Mum and Teddy at White Cliffs.

and friends. This grieving lasted several weeks, during which time Teddy's name was never mentioned.

To everyone's relief, two-year-old Rachel returned from hospital, fit and healthy, but she continually inquired as to Teddy's whereabouts.

May and Bill had separated only a few weeks prior to Teddy's death and May continually reminded us that our father was a good man. He loved us all. Beautiful glossy birthday cards reinforced this message. These were unfailingly sent to each of us, including May, along with personal cards at Christmas.

Off to school

On the first day at school in White Cliffs, I jumped the gun. I'd seen all the other kids going, including our cousins, the Rileys, and I knew what time they went. I thought all that mattered was to arrive and say to the teacher, 'Hey, look who you've got here. Let me get started.'

I'd remembered Roy and Doreen doing correspondence school in the big old tin kitchen we had at Willangie, and I had been to the school at Tibooburra for a few weeks but all I remember of that time was that I would be thumped by the school bully whenever I went to the toilet. I learned to wait until after playtime before asking permission to go to the loo. That didn't impress the teacher.

I knew there was a lot more to school than my experiences to date, so off I went to school without May having any idea where I'd gone. I was well-dressed, or so I thought, and I had gotten up early, washed and had breakfast. The main things I had prepared were my medals and crosses. I was such a proud little Catholic and I was sure that it would impress the teacher. I enjoyed being a Catholic because Father Carmine, a priest from Broken Hill, used to stay with us overnight at Coally Bore on his trips to Tibooburra. As well as enjoying his stories, he always brought along a large bag of boiled lollies.

I did not find out until years later that, noted in the column of religious denomination, where most of the students were listed as RCs (Roman Catholics) or ECs (Church of England), the Aboriginal students were simply listed as 'Abo'.

Arriving home that afternoon from my 'self enrolment', my joy was knocked sideways by the news that May needed more time to get my school clothes ready as well as see the teacher. I simply couldn't believe it.

Eventually, the day did come and I found school to be a good fun place. We played marbles and I was fairly good at that. Then one day May asked me how I had come to own so many marbles. When I told her I had won them, she said that it was wrong because that was gambling and gambling was a sin. Because of my Catholic conscience and Catholic guilt, and knowing that God knew that I was sinning, I wondered why He hadn't stopped me. He should have made me lose or hurt a finger or something – anything. I hated parting with all those beautiful marbles. I realised that the only way to get around this was to say lots of prayers when I was playing. I used to pray that the others would win from me but it didn't seem to help.

There was also cricket at school. It was played with a tennis ball that was old and shiny with all the fluff worn off. I had never played cricket before so when I was asked to go over to the men's cricket ground after school, I felt pretty proud. When I got home I asked May if I could join the boys and she said no. When I told her that we only played with a tennis ball I was allowed to go.

On my arrival at the ground I was surprised to see they had the men's gear out. There were big bats and pads and nice hard, shiny red balls. That made me feel so much better. There wouldn't be any need to put May straight about that. I hadn't told a lie at the time and I wasn't going to get hurt anyway.

I felt pretty good when it was my turn to bat. I walked out onto the cement pitch with the men's pads on – the tops of them came up to my groin. That didn't matter as I could still run. As it happened, running wasn't an option because one of the big boys, a real fast bowler, was bowling at me and I couldn't get the big bat up quick enough to hit anything. Before I knew it I got hit just above the eye. It didn't knock me over or cut me but soon a big lump appeared, which meant it would be better for me to wait until dark to go home because May was less likely to see it.

I had it all worked out. All I had to do was get my school clothes on before I went to bed each night and rush off to school early every morning until the swelling went away, and May would be pleased that I liked school so much.

Roy was home from hospital. He and Doreen would bring something for me to eat and I would offer to run any messages in the afternoons. I only did that for a few days and when it wasn't too bad, I combed my hair down over it. My secret was kept for a while until May felt the small lump there when she was going over my head for lice. I told her I must have bumped it on something.

Wanaaring

After almost a year, we were on the move to fresher pastures. This time we were to move to Wanaaring, a little town on the banks of the Paroo River, one hundred and twenty miles west of Bourke. This was the country close to where May had hunted and grown up. Sonny and Laurie, May's brothers, both had old but reliable motor lorries and they helped us. I don't remember much about getting ready to move, all I remember was the anticipation of the journey.

After an early start we were off to our new home. Us children had no idea what to expect but we were excited because the grown-ups kept talking about the river. I knew about creeks, which flooded sometimes but were mostly dry, and I also knew about big waterholes in certain places. Rivers, I was told, had water in them 'all the time'. Sometimes there would be big floods that washed fences away and my uncles would get the job of fixing them.

Having spent a year at White Cliffs, with the miles of glistening white quartz and hard clay dumps from the opal diggings, it was a great experience to journey through a hard but beautiful landscape. Gravel-bedded creeks, lined with ghost gums, wound through slopes of gibber-covered earth dotted with drought-stunted mulga and beefwood trees. There were miles of bare stony ridges merging into low sandhills between the hard scalded claypans.

We stopped by one of these claypans for lunch and stretched our weary legs. May showed us where our ancestors used to camp near these claypans in the years when they had water in them. Many of the bigger pans would hold water for months and the ground on the edges was clean for camping. The claypan was smooth and hard for dancing, and although the edges of the sandhills were soft they were solid enough to dig holes for cooking game.

Around these camping areas one would find relics of long ago days. There were grinding stones, shallow dishes, axes and spear-heads, and scrapers of many kinds; sometimes there was an old nulla nulla or boomerang. The old camping grounds were always of great interest and excitement for everyone.

Eventually, the family arrived at the Wanaaring Station billabong, about two miles from the town and the main river. There was a scramble to get down off the truck and have a good look at the bridge. It was the biggest bridge I had ever seen. We decided to walk across it just in case the truck loaded with all our belongings ran over the side.

On the eastern side of the billabong there were some small but healthy mulga trees scattered among the few needlewood and ironwood trees, as well as turpentine and hopbush scrub. The ground had a softness about it.

All went well and we were soon entering the town of Wanaaring. There was sand on both sides of the traffic-hardened road and it didn't look much like a town to me. There was a big house on the river side of the road, with a 'police station' sign hanging over the verandah. Directly across was a house with 'post office' painted on a big sign out the front. Right beside this was a horseyard with a wooden swinging gate.

A fence with its corner against the horseyard belonged to the pub. Next to that was vacant ground and around the back was the laundry or, as we called it, the washhouse. Further on there were empty bottles and a wood heap. In front of the wood heap were a couple of rooms built away from the main building where the cook used to sleep.

The hotel kitchen was on one corner of the main building and just beside it was a big water tank up on a stand. A windmill at the back of the police station filled the pub's tank and beside the hotel was a cottage where the bush nurse lived. We used to go there later on when we had sore eyes or a nasty cut, or something that May simply couldn't fix.

The store had a separate fence around it with a few fruit trees. Us kids soon found out that the apricots and peaches were the best we had ever tasted – probably because we knew we could get caught sneaking them through a hole in the corner of the fence.

Wanaaring post office and hotel stockyard during the 1939 flood of Paroo River.

Behind the hotel and scattered further north were a few houses but not as many as in White Cliffs. The school was the roof we had seen sticking out of the scrub on the way into town. It was set back off the main road which continued along the river.

We travelled another mile to a place on the river that May and her two brothers remembered from their previous visits, many years before. This was to be our home for the next fourteen years.

Our new home at Wanaaring was very different from White Cliffs and Tibooburra. The only other town we could remember was Broken Hill, where we had spent some time awaiting the births of Beulah and Eric, but we didn't count that as it was so big it must have been a city.

Wanaaring was tiny by comparison and there weren't any rocks or stones at all. It was all sandhills and was right on the Paroo, which when full was wide and fast flowing. There were big trees and lignum bushes, which we had not seen before. The strange smell of mud made my nostrils flare.

There were lots of birds flying about, some walking along the edge of the water picking, others twittering from branches. May and her brothers knew exactly where they were going. They knew a good spot, a nice clean flat piece of ground right near the bridge over the main channel of the river, on the road to Bourke.

It was a place where we could easily get down to the water to fill buckets whenever we needed to. We could see at once it was a good place to play, with no bushes or trees on the flat ground – formerly a Chinese garden of four acres. It bordered a waterhole on the eastern side and beyond the western boundary was a road on the edge of a low sandhill covered with turpentine and hopbush scrub.

On our first day, two tents were erected and within the next few days a pit toilet went up, covered with bush timber and enclosed with hessian chaff bags. It had no roof, only logs that were placed across the edge of the hole as a floor. It was pretty basic.

On the third day we were greeted by one of the biggest dust storms I'd ever experienced. The dust clouds could be seen rolling in for quite a while before it arrived. The black and dark yellow clouds churned and rolled, darkening the sky and bringing sand from as far away as the Simpson. We had seen these dust storms before, so we knew to expect the strange calm before the storm arrived.

Strong relentless winds followed the swirling gusts, which lifted sand, dust and grit to form an ocean of dust that would eventually settle in faraway places. The adults packed food, blankets and a tarpaulin. We left the tents and took shelter on the eastern side of the river, under the protection of the strong lapunya trees and the thick bushy lignum foliage. We stayed until sunset when it subsided and then returned to our new home.

At that stage the camp was temporary as far as buildings were concerned. Laurie and Sonny busied themselves re-erecting the tents and tidying up. They started to build a bough shed and they cut and carted all the required timber with the help of us children. We all joined in digging up the wire netting from around the old garden site. It was submerged from years of sand blowing in from the desert. The netting was stretched over the timber frame to prevent the leaves of the small tree branches from falling through. There was unlimited hopbush scrub nearby and it served well as a windbreak on the western side of the shed.

Sonny and Laurie were confident that May, now in her mid-thirties, would manage with the help of her six children and seventeen-year-old Myrtle. They soon made preparations to return to their places of work. Before Sonny and Laurie took their leave, they ensured that there was a good supply of wood and did a shopping excursion with May to the expensive but only store Wanaaring had. They did a big buy, as big as their money would allow, and took it back on one of the lorries.

Once they left, all we had in the line of transport was an old pushbike, which I'd learnt to ride at poor Roy's expense. That provided faster transport for getting small supplies. When May wanted a bigger order the old cane perambulator, which had been bought for Teddy, was used. Over the years we kept modifying the pram as it slowly disintegrated.

Everything that could be carried in it, that fitted on it or that could be dragged behind was thrown in and treated the same. There was no need to be careful with the modified version. It still served as grocery transport even when we later got the spring carts. It was easier to run the two-mile round trip with the pram than to yoke a horse and it was more fun – not that May always thought it funny when we arrived home with leaking flour and sugar bags, or the remains of a cracked sauce bottle.

Improvements to the home were an ongoing task. Materials for the more substantial dwellings came in the form of four-gallon petrol tins, which were in fair supply around town and along main roads. All petrol in those days came in a wooden case containing two square four-gallon tins. As motorists emptied the contents into their vehicle, the empty receptacle would be tossed to the side of the road. So every time we went wood carting or hunting there would be a little more building material to be taken home.

We would cut the ends out and split each down the side. The tins were beaten out flat and laid in readiness for them to be tied in shingled layers; fixed as the roof and walls to make the kitchen and later the bedrooms. There would sometimes be so many tins that we were unable to carry them. They would be left in a sheltered place to be collected at another time. The timber could not be left lying for too long as it would be harder to cut and bore, and it was also inclined to split while being worked. With May's determination, building knowledge and driving organisational skills, it was not long before our home took shape. We were working towards living in a solid weatherproof dwelling.

The aim was to build a pitched roofed hut, about twenty feet long by ten feet wide, to serve as a kitchen and storeroom. When that was completed a similar-sized room was added for May and, later, one for the girls. The boys felt they didn't need the same amount of privacy as required by the girls.

Some of the bedrooms had opened wheat bags on the floor that had been pegged down with wire staples, but the kitchen had too much traffic so the bags would not last long. After we got beds that were movable we could change the position of the bedroom furniture and redirect the traffic before the bagged floor became too worn.

A garden was needed so the tin gathering did not stop there. The flattened tins were tied to railings to form a garden enclosure. As time went on more timber was used to erect a goatyard. Everyone worked hard.

The garden

Anybody with ideas of starting a garden would most likely begin with a pump to provide water. Not May. There was water in the nearby river and a team of strong-limbed kids. All she had to do was make a few buckets from an endless supply of petrol tins and that was the beginning of our vegetable garden.

In the early stages we used those buckets to carry the water up steps cut in the riverbank. As May had an eye for improving things, it was not long before a small semi-rotary hand pump arrived in the mail from Bourke. With some new couplings it was linked to the river with piping that had been discarded from the original garden as well as one further downstream, abandoned many years before.

We later purchased a bigger double-action pump and some extra piping, followed by a small windmill and a thousand-gallon tank. All we had to do was pump the water into a forty-four-gallon drum set into the ground at the highest point and irrigation drains were cut to run water from it, to wherever it was needed. Soon, in no time at all, there was a flourishing market garden, which was to supply the town and many travellers along the river.

ABOVE *May and Janet in the shade house at Wanaaring.*

BELOW *May and her brother Frank in the garden at Wanaaring.*

May believed in watering the garden in the mornings during the summer months. She felt that water on hot ground in the afternoons would scald the roots of some of the tender, sensitive vegetables. Her theory seemed to work as our garden always produced strong healthy vegies.

However, we had a theory about the tomatoes. We were never able to find a half-ripe one. There was suspicion among us and we thought we were outsmarting each other. If one of us kids was seen in the garden at non-watering times, others would either spy on him or her from an unseen place or go and confront the suspect, closely examining the bushes which never produced a ripe tomato. Amazingly, every time a drover or traveller arrived they were always able to buy a few nice, big red juicy tomatoes. We eventually discovered that May knew exactly when to take the fruit from the vines and these were ripened in a large biscuit tin which was kept in her room. This one room, of course, was out of bounds.

May had a very good method of water clearing. Water was pumped into forty-four-gallon drums and mixed with Epsom salts or a couple of shovels of ashes from our cooking fires. The clearing process was usually effective in a matter of two or three hours. Of course the drums had to be regularly cleared of sediment.

The drums were usually set two-thirds into the ground to be low enough for us to get water from them without having to reach above waist height and risk muscle strain. The clearing meant baling as much sediment as possible, then splashing in clean water and repeating the process several times. As a final touch an old towel or cloth would be used to wipe the lower half and bottom clean. During good rainfall seasons the river water was fairly clear and suitable for drinking.

The big box swamps or gilgais often had water in them for most of the year, attracting wildlife, which meant easier hunting. We knew the countryside after a short time at Wanaaring so when we wanted to head off into the bush for a day's hunting,

May would ask one of the local graziers which paddock we could go into. Naturally they would offer a paddock with no sheep.

We would hitch the horses to the wagonette, which May had bought from a drover going out of business, and load some tucker and water on board. One of the adults would mount a saddle horse and we always took a couple of reliable kangaroo dogs.

More goats

Mrs Grey, the proprietor of the Wanaaring hotel, had a herd of goats, which she wanted to dispose of. A deal was soon negotiated and May agreed to take a young male and several breeding nannies along with whatever kids were afoot. With close attention, the goats soon accepted their new territory and enclosing the kids at night ensured the mob did not stray. Later, we acquired a couple of pigs and some fowls. In addition, drum nets were made to catch fish for our dinners.

Neither the goat herd nor the horses took long to establish their territorial grazing areas. In no time we began supplying goats milk to the hotel and police station. Some townspeople bought vegetables from us as well as drovers or passers-by with sheep and cattle bound for the railheads of Broken Hill or Bourke.

The drovers added to our growing number of livestock when there were unplanned births of lambs or calves, which usually had to be killed because they were unable to survive the hazardous journey. We used to take these youngsters and rear them on goats milk until they were able to fend for themselves. When the calves

ABOVE *May and niece Mary Riley leave Wanaaring to fetch horses from Coally Bore, a 400-mile round trip.*
BELOW *Horses and goat herd with sheep and poddy calf at Wanaaring.*

May holding camel's head while Rupert Crowe applies tar to mange area. His son Henry and Mary Riley look on.

were old enough they were sold, while the lambs stayed on with the goats and eventually provided extra money from their wool clips once a year. We never sold mutton to people requesting meat. If they wanted meat from us it would be goat.

It wasn't long before May left Myrtle in charge while she and an older niece, Mary Riley, went back to Coally Bore to bring back May's horses. Bill had been looking after them. His eyes had not troubled him during that period so he had stayed on at the bore. It was almost a four-hundred-mile round trip to get the horses; however, riding in the bush was the part of life that May and Mary enjoyed the most.

The horses they brought back were watched closely until they settled down. There was fairly good grazing at our end of the common, the river being the eastern boundary so our horses usually grazed not far from where we lived. When they accepted that part of the country as their territory we were able to graze them further afield.

Spring cart

May's younger brother, Frank, and Mary Riley later came over from White Cliffs with another couple of horses. In country that was new to them, these horses, too, had to be kept close and watched until they settled.

Everything gradually developed. The arrival of a spring cart, which made life so much easier, had been a stroke of luck due entirely to the hidden generosity of one of our neighbours. Bill Stalley, a local grazier, came and asked May if she would be so kind as to let him leave his spring cart with her for safekeeping and use, until he was able to have it taken to his property on Tinappagee Station, twenty-odd miles upriver. May agreed. It was a more convenient vehicle for wood carting and small hunting trips, requiring only one horse.

Bill was careful not to patronise. He respected everyone and had a bonding with Aboriginal people that stemmed from his childhood. He and an Aboriginal child, fostered by his parents, were christened in the same ceremony by a preacher named Captain Black. He was captain of a river steamer named 'Hero'.

From that day on, those two playmates were known as Bill Stalley and Hero Black. When Hero Black reached adulthood, he rejoined his traditional people and became a respected leader. His brother Bill, being from a grazing family, prospered as a well-to-do land-holder. Despite their differences, these men maintained a kinship throughout their long lives.

Every time May saw Bill Stalley, she would ask when he was going to get his cart and he always replied that he would come and get it one day. That cart was handy for so many things. There were wonderful hunting days in it and at other times we would yoke a horse and find straight timbers for the uprights of the house or slender ones for rafters. These would be lugged home, bark removed, cut into required lengths and then put aside until there were enough to complete a wall or room.

There was always wood to be carted and when word was received from a drover that he had a couple of newborn calves, it was easier to carry them home in the spring cart.

Friendship

I noticed little of the settling-in to Wanaaring and I didn't give much thought as to how it all happened. However, we had not been in the new place long when the local police officer paid us a surprising visit. Senior Constable George Tarrant let May know that he was available should there be an emergency or if May needed information about local issues. He also noticed that she was a keen horsewoman.

May explained that she had grown up with horses and that her father had done a lot of horse breaking while she was his mainstay. The policeman smiled and said he wanted May to meet his wife, Edna, as she was also a horsewoman.

During this period, May had introduced herself to the storekeeper and post office people. She had also made the time to meet the bush nurse and schoolteacher. The schoolteacher resided at the police station, so it was when she was there that she met the policeman's wife, Edna Tarrant. From that day on, the two women became friends.

Edna Tarrant was as keen a horsewoman as May, so they often went riding together and both participated at the local race meetings. There was never a ladies race on the program as there were not enough women riders. Regardless of this situation and the social implications, May and Edna, along with Aileen Jackson, a grazier's daughter from Wongareena Station, competed successfully among the men. It gave the Wanaaring race meetings an added flavour and the little town had at least three competent and respected local lady riders at all the meetings.

A welcome hand was soon proffered by some of the locals. Mrs Grey, who owned the hotel and little grocery store, agreed to allow May a monthly account. Then another local grazier called one day and introduced himself. His name was Henry Gibbons. He let May know that if there was anything he or his sons could do, to let them know. Henry Gibbons was in the process of buying Wanaaring Station from Sidney Kidman. He had put in a new manager, Les Gardener. Les came from Thargominda in Queensland and apparently was a decent sort of bloke. So whenever May wanted to go hunting on the property all she had to do was ask.

School at Wanaaring

To begin with, us kids hadn't gotten to know any of the other children about town but the incident of the bailing-up of the local Bambricks on the bridge changed that. The Bambricks owned Moolaka Station, four miles up the river from town, and when there was a fair bit of water in the river, they used to have to cross via the bridge. When the river was low they crossed about half a mile above where we lived.

The bail-up on the bridge by us was a pretty bold move, or so we thought. Roy and I stood in the middle of the main channel bridge as the Bambrick children approached. We thought they would be scared of us new kids and tell us everything we wanted to know about everyone as well as how many kids went to school. It was the marking of our territory. However, the Bambrick kids didn't scare that easily. They enjoyed the challenge of rights to the road. We were satisfied that we had extracted their names and other local information from them, only to learn later that none of the names were correct or the information accurate. So, until we got to know them better and became really good friends, the bridge bail-up was a topic us Hunt kids avoided.

The first day of school at Wanaaring came soon enough. We found ourselves being packed off to school. May got us up and announced that it was time to go. She told us that the teacher, Mr Rose, knew all about us. She explained that she had already met him and we would recognise him because he was the only adult at the school. The couple of teachers I'd previously met seemed alright, so things might not be that bad. I was unsure of the kids, although I wasn't afraid to have a fight with anyone now that I was nine years old.

Off we went, all spruced up. May made sure we were clean, tidy and well-mannered. While it was good to be dressed up, there was some discomfort at having to keep a shirt tucked in and buttoned up, bootlaces tied and your 'pleases' and 'thank yous' in check. Starting school at Wanaaring was not the same as at White Cliffs. Going to school then had been a novelty. This time I was prepared for the worst.

There were no other local kids that we knew as we hadn't met any, apart from the Bambricks, and we just waved whenever we passed them. There was much laughter and teasing as we set out to school that day. There were many things to occupy our minds during the mile to school.

We walked across the old garden site, then through the town itself. We knew we would have to go past the front of the pub, then the post office and police station. Often there would be people gathered on the hotel verandah or in front of the post office and, because we were new, they would look at us.

If we didn't go that way, we would have to go around the back and that meant getting too close to houses and people might have said something unpleasant if they thought we were stickybeaking. We didn't know what these Wanaaring white people were like. We did know that everywhere else we'd been, the white people always kept an eye on Aboriginals.

We entered the town proper, then on through the quarter mile of hopbush scrub and along a narrow worn track, which led to the school. The schoolhouse was enclosed by a post and rail fence system with a rusty cyclone gate. The fence was to keep out straying horses and cattle, which grazed in the area during the spring months when grass was plentiful. Cautiously passing through the narrow gate, we surveyed the area and crept onto the verandah, which ran across the front and down both sides of one big classroom.

We thought we had better see if there was anyone else inside. Peeping over the windowsill confirmed an empty school. We were early. What a good start to the day. We sat on the edge of the verandah in the morning sun to wait. It wasn't long before there were voices in the direction of the town. Some other kids were arriving and the tension rose within us.

As the other students entered the clearing and saw the little group of strangers on the verandah, their laughter and chatter abruptly stopped. They froze. Six or so of them looked up, down, away, then quickly turned and vanished into the scrub from where they had just emerged. We had never had anyone run away from us before. It wasn't long before a man, with an open-necked shirt and a hatless high forehead that gleamed in the sun, appeared and entered the school ground surrounded by the runaway kids. Mr Rose called out a greeting, 'Good morning. You must be the Hunt children. I met with your mother the other day. Welcome to Wanaaring.' We didn't say a word.

School took on a different perspective for me at Wanaaring, not only because I was older but also I had some idea of what was expected. I was stuck on being boss drover so I accepted that I had to learn the essentials of reading, writing and arithmetic. I would have to tolerate all the other stuff, which I considered to be baggage.

I liked Mr Rose and under his guidance I learned quite a lot. He was an easygoing and likable kind of bloke. We learned that we could talk to him about anything. He always had a big fire going in the schoolroom during winter and in the summer he would take us out to sit on the verandah or under the shade of a big pepper tree. He would always say 'g'day' if we met him in the town and he wasn't one of those flashy whites. The other teachers who came along later were also pretty good.

Only one teacher used to hit the grog and be cranky when he had to come to school after a heavy drinking binge on the weekend. He also used to teach Sunday School and one day he caned me with the centre stick of a date palm and put blood blisters all over my hands. The following Sunday he arrived to take us to Sunday School and May confronted him about the extent of my punishment. He replied, 'That's nothing to what another kid's got coming to him.' May promptly told him she thought he was too cruel to teach us about God. We didn't go to Sunday School any more and that suited us just fine.

The relocation

During the 1930s, while we were settling into our new home, the government was a party to a sinister move that was taking place. The oppression that had been brought about by the White Australia policy of that era was developed further. The New South Wales government had introduced the Aborigines Protection Act in 1909, which resulted in an Aborigines Welfare Board. The regulations of the board were presided over by police in country towns and those officers were always supported by the local white majority. The laws made life very difficult for all Aboriginal people and particularly for those in mixed marriages. They governed people's lives and no Aboriginal person was unaffected.

This 'protection' board had organised the transport of all those living on their traditional homeland at Tibooburra to Brewarrina Mission Station, a place they had never heard of. They forced women, children and the elderly to get onto trucks with nothing more than a blanket. They were told that if they didn't do this then their children would be taken away to children's homes, which left the families with no option.

Tibooburra people in transit to Brewarrina Mission.

The first we heard of this forced relocation was when trucks rumbled across the loose planks on the river bridge near our place. There emerged two of the biggest motor trucks we had ever seen. Two Aboriginal men came over and were met by May. One of them she had known as a child. He recognised May and greeted her. He explained that they were taking the Tibooburra mob to Brewarrina Mission on the Darling River.

May was aghast. She knew that it could easily have been us if we had still lived in Tibooburra. Because our father was white we were not able to live among our own extended family and that may have saved us from this trauma. Eventually the bewildered group began the long journey into country they had never been to.

When the working men arrived home in Tibooburra for their usual monthly break, they found their families gone and their camps deserted. The true courage of those Malyangapa people came to the fore at this time.

A meeting was held and it was clear to the men that this relocation had been a directive of the Aborigines Protection Board. They had never really trusted it, but had not thought of it acting in this devastating way.

On their way through Wanaaring these men called at our home and told us the story of what had happened when they returned to find their families gone. It went something like this:

'Well, what we gonna do now?'

'S'pose we go to the gungy (police). He tell us what happened to our people, where they gone?'

About a dozen of these confused, frustrated and angry people then went to the police station to be met by two police officers who gruffly greeted the small crowd.

'Well, what you mob want?'

'We want to know what happen to our people? Where they gone?'

'They gone to the mission, that big mission at Brewarrina. You mob gotta go there, too.'

'But this our place here. This our home. We belong to this country, we got no right to just go to those other fellas' place. This is the land we belong to.'

'Listen,' said the sergeant. 'That's all blackfella stuff. That's all finished now. You gotta do what the Board say. The Aboriginal Protection Board gonna look after all you mob now, and you got to do what they tell you. They put you all on these missions. That way they know where everybody is. That way they can keep an eye on you all and look after you, make your kids go to school and stop all that bloody blackfella talk you teaching your kids. That's all rubbish lingo now. Everyone got to talk the proper way now, like I talk.'

'I'll give you directions,' continued the sergeant. 'I'll show you how to get to Brewarrina. I'll give you all some rations for the road. But that's it, you got to go and keep going.'

'We'll keep goin' alright,' they replied. 'We'll keep goin'. We gonna get our people back, and we got to come back here to this place. This is our proper place.'

The sergeant ignored that last remark. 'You blokes know that road that goes sunrise from here, that cut line. Well, that goes straight to Wanaaring on the Paroo River, that's a hundred and seventy miles from here. There's a policeman there. He'll tell you anything you want to know about the road and water, and he will make sure you keep going. No muckin' around and makin' trouble. Then you keep going the same way, another hundred and twenty miles to Bourke. That's a big town on the Darling River, from there it's only about sixty miles up the river to Brewarrina.

'You all come up here tomorrow and I'll give you your last lot of rations. I'll ring up that policeman at Wanaaring and tell him you are on your way and you got to keep going. We don't want any trouble. You know what we do if you play up. So you just get going.'

These men had to make their own way to Brewarrina to be with their families. They had to use their own transport, whatever they had – buggies and horses, camels, an old motor vehicle.

So this sad and angry group began the long journey into country they had never been to, a place they had not even heard of before. All of them had personal belongings – musical instruments, saddles and clothes, special boomerangs and stock-whips – at their places of employment but they had decided to leave them. They thought there was no point in going back for their possessions because they believed that they would soon return with their families. They had no intention of being pushed off into another place that belonged to strange people.

This was where they belonged and they would return as soon as they were able to get their families together.

Myrtle had begun work at the Wanaaring hotel as a domestic, cleaning rooms and working in the kitchen as a cook's offsider. For the first time in her life, she had her own spending money. Her pride and joy was getting her pay packet every week, which enabled her to buy clothes from travelling hawkers and little gifts for the younger members of the family. It was some independence for Myrtle and we all looked up to her.

Myrtle lived for many years helping us and it was so cruel when she was suddenly struck with rheumatic fever and taken to the hospital in Bourke. As much as we were going to miss her, we believed that it would only be a short time before she came back home, as had been the case with Roy. Myrtle had never been inside a hospital, not even as a visitor, so it was totally foreign.

There were people with coloured uniforms and caps and some with starched veils that resembled wooden wings of model aeroplanes. The smell of the bush was many miles away. Disinfectant and ether were the only smells. There was an air of seriousness and at meal times a trolley would be wheeled around in silence.

Myrtle's main comfort was that she would soon be getting better and after a while she believed that she would be able to go home. Although she was never told whether she was getting better or not, she was sure that she would because she was in a place where doctors made sick people well again. Roy had had rheumatic fever and had gotten better.

Myrtle's stay in hospital was lonely and some of our relatives called in to see her on their way to Brewarrina to visit Uncle Laurie's wife's people, who were a part of that terrible shift from Tibooburra. Myrtle knew it was not possible to get a visit from us at Wanaaring.

Tinappagee adventure

May decided that we would attend a gathering at Tinappagee Station. Her brother Laurie and his family would be there, and there would be other people and children we knew but many we didn't know. Rather than pack six kids and our food and camping gear into one cart, May thought it better to take two. We had a couple of good fat carthorses called Dot and Starnch, and May would ride on her favourite stockhorse. This way the trip would be comfortable and old Bill Stalley might like us to leave his cart there while we had the chance. As it turned out, he refused, stating our cart was much smaller than his and that May could buy it from him if she wished. The sale did eventually take place and the price was a token amount.

A family friend, Arthur Crowe, was living with us at the time. He was a happy-go-lucky type of bloke who appeared to have aged ahead of his years as he had been affected by the medical condition St Vitus' dance. He had a speech impediment coupled with the struggle to pronounce words in his second language, English. None of these things deterred Arthur from his zest for living and sense of humour.

Arthur was happy to take care of our home while we were away. There was no better caretaker. Arthur and his brother Rupert were, in Aboriginal way, nephews of my grandmother, Hannah Quayle, and they always called May 'sister'.

May organised my brother Eric, cousin Keith Quayle and myself into one cart. Keith was Laurie's son and was staying with us at Wanaaring so that he could attend school. Doreen, Beulah and Rachel were in the other cart, with Doreen in charge. May's mount was a saddle horse, which enabled her to move about and keep an eye on everything.

There was an excited feeling when the traces tightened and the cart moved in response to a slap on the rump and a gee-up. There was a slow walk away from the camp and a farewell wave to Arthur. As Bill had taught us, it was important to give the horses time to settle into the feel of the harness and to make sure that they were comfortable with each strap and chain as well as the weight of the vehicle.

Horses always seemed to go through the same ritual when moving into the collar to pull their load. There was a low grinding sound as the sand was squeezed out from under the iron tyres, followed by the cracking of small sticks and the occasional stone being crunched. The chump, chump of horses' hooves shifted to a more solid clop, clop as we moved onto the harder ground of windswept, sun-baked country and away from the sandhills.

The garden had been well watered the night before which was contrary to May's normal custom of watering in the mornings. May was not going to ask Arthur to do any watering while we were away. It was good of him to care for the animals, and the garden could survive the days we were gone. It was not hot at that time of year.

After about two hours May called a halt in the shade of a box tree and we got the tucker box down. There was the usual scuffle to see what she had packed for the stopover and to get what we always imagined would be the choicest bits. Although that was never the case, we never gave up looking. When May decided the horses had had sufficient rest, we were off again. By now, we were going into strange territory. We were off our own stomping ground.

We arrived at Laurie's camp in the afternoon. The box trees cast long shadows that formed a soft cool carpet interspersed with splashes of golden light. The dogs that were tied to pegs and tree branches reefed on their chains and barked in excitement. There were the usual mixed breeds but many were sheep dogs and staghound crosses, and best used for hunting.

We had our own camp dogs, of course. Janet, our German-collie bitch, and Norm, a blue heeler, as well as two kangaroo dogs tethered to the axles of the carts. They seemed content to stay put and observe the situation. There were several tents, lean-tos and brush-covered gunyahs (small rough huts) spaced at distances allowing privacy for each family. Each had its own fireplace that consisted mainly of galleys of hanging rails for water buckets and camp ovens sheltered by sheets of corrugated iron and brush.

Further on was the red roof of the station homestead and this was prominent above the high fence of old-man saltbushes, wattles and other shrubs. May identified Laurie and his wife Bub's camp, and the cry went out. Everyone came running and the introductions were on. There were more relations than we knew what to do with. Some were blood relations, others were culturally related or extended family. Some had come down from Queensland.

A couple of the men offered to unyoke the horses and take them to water and grass. I shyly conceded and joined the hugs and handshakes of family and friends.

There was the smell of burning logs and the dry leaves of eucalypts as people stoked their fires and began cooking their evening meal. The smell of grilled kangaroo and emu wafted through the air. There was a comforting atmosphere about the place and there did not appear to be any divisions or boundaries. It felt like coming home.

The night crept upon us unnoticed. There was much talking, laughing and moving around; people were mixing, mingling, introducing and being introduced. 'This is your cousin, your aunty, your uncle. This one, my brother's new wife, that one over there, you can call that one granny.' That's the way we were welcomed into the group. There was talk of a corroboree later. That was alright with me as I'd seen and participated in corroborees in White Cliffs and Tibooburra when I was younger.

Mum made our beds in the spring carts so as to keep the bedclothes off the ground. Just a few green leaves and hessian for mattresses and we settled into deep slumber. The long day and the excitement of meeting everyone had left us exhausted.

It was a great few days we spent at Tinappagee. The strangeness soon disappeared and we went along with whatever was taking place – playing, learning new games, resting, hunting and swimming. Swimming was a special one. We were now living on the river but had never been swimming in it before. We only knew about the waterholes along the gum-lined creek at Coally after heavy rain caused flooding. There was much to learn and such a short time to enjoy it. I was confident that I would learn to swim as soon as we returned home to the riverbanks at Wanaaring.

We experienced the learning of a lifetime in just a few days. Then regrettably it was time to go. The night before we were to leave was a late one with adults sitting around the fires, yarning and laughing. We were allowed to stay up late and as the night wore on people drifted off in ones and twos to their camps. The fires were no longer being stoked other than to drop a large log on, to provide red-hot coals for the morning.

Despite the late night, there was much activity the next morning. The sun peeped over the tree-lined Paroo and I could feel life being breathed into a new day. Our horses were kept in the station's horse paddock and were easily rounded up and brought to the camps and yoked for the return journey. There were hugs, kisses and handshakes. A box brownie camera was found, focussed and clicked, and photos taken to hold the memories of that wondrous occasion. Then with a click of the tongue and a slap of the reins, we were on our way.

Mishap

We had planned to find a nice clean spot to have a break on the trip home. All went well for about an hour with May riding beside us boys in the lead cart. We were halfway across a large claypan when suddenly the stillness was broken by screams from the girls, snorting from a bucking Dot and the cracking of her hooves against the front of the cart.

Dot was making every effort to free herself from the cart and her harness. She'd been frightened by the breaking of the harness back band, which had allowed the shafts of the vehicle to drop to the ground.

May galloped back but was helpless to intervene until Dot had freed herself. Eventually the shafts speared into the ground and the cart was catapulted over the frantically bucking Dot. The two dogs that were attached to the rear of the cart were swung over and landed under the upturned cart.

We were too afraid to look at the girls for a while. So much had happened so quickly, and the scene appeared to have unfolded in slow motion. My three sisters were lying like dolls, flung from the overturned cart and scattered across the ground.

By the time I'd turned our horse around and tied the reins to the wheel to hold him, May was on her knees beside the girls. Beulah and Rachel were soon on their feet and ran to Doreen, who was the only one not to move.

'My leg is broken,' she whispered. There was no doubt about that. Her right foot was turned in the opposite direction to the way she was facing. May had no first-aid experience but common sense prevailed. She held Doreen's injured foot firmly on the ground and encouraged her to turn her whole body over to be in line with her foot. I will never forget Doreen's face as the brave twelve year old gritted her teeth, closed her eyes and squeezed the tears from between her lids. Not a sound was made as she obeyed May's instructions to have her leg set in place.

Boards were pulled from the side of our tucker box and applied as splints, bound in place with strips torn from bedsheets. We all did our bit of quiet crying after Doreen was placed in the other cart.

May was able to catch the offending Dot and lead her beside the remaining transport as we made our way to Lenroy Station some five miles further on. There was no telephone at Lenroy. There was, however, a car but all the men were away and the property owner's teenage daughter, Vera, said she had never driven the car alone. She always had her father or one of her brothers with her, but this was an emergency and Vera volunteered to try.

About to depart Uncle Laurie's camp at Tinappagee –
just before the accident that broke Doreen's leg.

May had only ever driven a T-model Ford. She had never driven a geared car of any type. So Doreen was transferred from the cart to the car and made the trip of another twelve miles to Wanaaring. The bush nurse made her as comfortable as possible. They had to wait until the return of the local police officer as he had been visiting outlying properties. He had the only reliable means of transport for taking a patient over the unformed road to Bourke, which was a hundred and twenty miles away.

Accompanied by the bush nurse, the police officer transported Doreen to Bourke hospital. Fortunately, despite the pain and the discomfort of the swelling, the x-rays showed that the leg had been perfectly set by May. All that was required was plaster and time to heal the break.

The only comfort for Doreen was that she found herself beside Myrtle, whom she had not seen for some time. Both were bedridden but at least they were together. In that strange environment, the girls were a support for each other. Myrtle especially found great strength in the companionship of Doreen.

The two girls shared a lot in the following days and tired themselves out with their reminiscences. Then one night Myrtle just kept on talking and as much as Doreen wanted to listen, sleep kept getting in the way. As she dozed, Doreen could hear Myrtle's voice fading. Doreen wanted to stay awake but couldn't. Doreen was awakened some time later by Myrtle shouting, 'Aunty May! Aunty May! I want Aunty May. Please get Aunty May.' Then she fell silent.

It was a silence unlike anything Doreen had ever experienced. The night staff quickly came to Myrtle's bed and a few minutes later wheeled it away. Doreen knew that she would never see Myrtle again. Turning her face deep into her pillow, she sobbed herself into a state of exhaustion and eventually slept.

For Doreen, the days and nights from then on just dragged. Her whole body seemed empty – she no longer wanted to eat, or talk to or see anyone. She wanted to get home to Mum and family. They must be suffering, too, and she knew there was strength there, back home.

All was in order at the Hunt camp, everyone getting on with their morning chores when the same car which had taken Doreen away to Bourke turned off the main road and eased to a halt just a few yards away from where we all gathered. It was natural for us to stop whatever we were doing as the arrival of the local police officer usually meant something was wrong. On this occasion, as usual, May seemed to know what that something was.

May and George Tarrant stopped a few paces apart, murmuring a low 'Morning' to each other. Without another word the police officer put his arm around her shoulders and we gathered around as they sat on two petrol tins we used as chairs. May reached out to hold us all as she chokingly whispered, 'It's Myrtle. We've lost poor dear Myrtle. She's passed away.'

Senior Constable Tarrant was generally a stern type of person. But on this day he emanated an aura of soft gentleness. He rose and walked a few paces away to allow us to express and share our grief in comfort and privacy. It is the only time I can ever recall seeing him obviously distressed. He waited beside his car until May was sufficiently composed to go to him.

'Mr Tarrant, thank you for bringing us that message, although it was bad news. We will be alright now. Me and the kids will have a good cry. Then we can talk about anything I have to do.'

The officer left, promising that his wife would come later to see if there was anything she could offer.

'Oh Mum, what are we going to do now? And what about Doreen? Is she going to be alright?'

We were all distraught and May reassured us, 'Doreen will be alright, and be home soon. She's not seriously sick like Myrtle was. She has only got a broken leg and that will get better and strong enough for her to come home in a couple of weeks. Myrtle has gone to heaven and she will be company for little Teddy. She can look after him.'

Later in the day we heard the call, 'You there May? It's me, Edna.'

The tall, dark-haired Edna Tarrant had walked the mile from town. The two women embraced, then sat in silence for a long time.

The claypan dances were not regular events. They occurred when a few people were around and someone suggested that they all go up to May's place to see if they could have a dance-up. They got all the old-time records and played them on the gramophone. The word soon spread and people would arrive after dinner. Blankets would be brought for the children, who usually tired themselves out long before the night was over.

There were two strict rules at these dances. Firstly, there were no hard-soled boots or shoes to be worn on the earthen-floor dance area because if the surface was broken it became dusty. Waltzes, barn dances and the schottische were popular choices. May excelled at the sword dance and was always keen to teach the young ones.

Others specialised in the Charleston, and in those days most people were inclined to do a bit of tap-dancing. Tap shoes would be worn and a specially made wooden platform would be unveiled. This platform was kept safely out of the way in case someone decided to use it for kindling.

At our place there was a nice even piece of ground between

Dance hall in Wanaaring.

the kitchen and living areas. It was always hard due to the regular barefoot and sandshoe traffic passing through. We also used to throw the clean wastewater on it like we did the other earthen-floor rooms. There were never any activities allowed which might cause it to become uneven.

The second rule was no alcohol. As well as it being illegal for Aboriginal people to have alcohol, it was also deeply shameful. Drunks got into trouble with the police and made fools of themselves. They were considered bad role models. If anyone had alcohol they had to keep away from the entertainment area. Sometimes you would see a couple of cigarettes glowing in the distance, a couple of hundred yards away from our house. They would be the drinkers and should the intoxicated ones decide to have a closer look, they would always keep a respectable distance from the crowd.

May's brothers Laurie and Jack worked as contract fencers and shearers in the Wanaaring district, so when they came to town to replenish their grocery supplies or had time-out between jobs, they would happily join in the claypan dances.

Most people were able to play an instrument of some kind. Mouth organs and Jew's harps seemed to appear from almost everybody's shirt pocket. May and her brothers played the accordion and also the banjo and the bones. In the absence of real bones, they substituted spoons. Most of us played the gum leaf. These were never to be forgotten occasions when our home throbbed with life and the happiness of sharing what we had with other people.

Success and racism

May was always on guard against racism and her recipe was simple. 'Don't ever put yourself above anyone else and don't allow yourself to be put beneath anyone either.' We had to keep clean, tidy and honest and she assured us that there was always someone who would respect you for that. She taught us that we had to have respect for ourselves.

May was strong on respect and we knew the importance of it. Naturally we wanted respect from the white people also. However, we were continually made aware of the material differences and we learned to measure success in terms of materialism. Our traditional and spiritual teachings were ridiculed, even by the Catholic church. We lived in absolute awe of the god taught to us by the church.

In addition, there were local laws whereby people tried to prevent us from going to dance halls and cinemas or entering into sporting events. When we were travelling someplace, often people we didn't know would stop and ask, 'And just where the hell do think you're going?' In the early days most, out of fear, would offer an explanation usually by admitting the truth – whatever that was.

Edna Tarrant was a competent pianist, who provided most of the music for the regular Saturday night dances at Wanaaring. When she realised the excellent musical skills of her Aboriginal friends she soon enlisted their support and asked them to play. We had never bothered about the dances in the town and had just enjoyed our occasional get-togethers on the claypan.

We never even thought of asking a white girl to dance. And, of course, white men never asked any Aboriginal women I knew to dance either. I never saw this as anything remarkable until one day at the post office, I overheard a conversation.

'Who's playing at the dance tonight?'

'Oh, I suppose it will be Edna Tarrant, May Hunt and her brothers. They provide good music.'

'Can't we get by without having those niggers in the hall?'

Well, that was the signal for me to take the news home to May. We had been treated with so much respect since arriving at Wanaaring. May relayed those remarks to Edna, who was quick to express her disapproval to the offender and pointedly suggested that his presence at the dance was 'not essential'.

Court business

There was an occasion when May, Eric, Rachel and Cyril were driving the goats and pet sheep off the bridge near home. The postmaster, who also owned the town's general store, came speeding along in his 1930s touring car on his way to visit his lady friend, several miles up the river. By the time he had noticed the goats on the road, he was unable to stop and ended up among the herd, knocking over one of the animals. Fortunately the goat was not seriously hurt but instead of an apology, the postmaster launched into a tirade of obscenities.

'Hey gin, git yer snotty-nosed kids, yer goats and those bloody mangy dogs off the road or I'll bloody well run yers over.'

'I beg your pardon,' said May as she steadily approached the car.

'I said gin, git yer bloody kids and dogs off the road.'

'I thought that's what you said,' answered May as the back of her hand smacked across the postmaster's face. With a roar of the motor, he quickly drove off.

The children chattered excitedly. 'Bet he won't tell his girlfriend what happened when he gets to her place. That's where he's goin', he goes up there very day. Mum, he might go and tell the policeman and then Mr Tarrant will have to put you in gaol. We wouldn't be able to go to school if you were locked up, would we?'

'Don't get too excited at a chance to miss out on going to school. I won't be getting locked up. The postmaster's not silly enough to tell Mr Tarrant or anyone else what happened to him,' replied May.

The children told the story to everyone at school. It then spread throughout the community as the joke of the week. A few days passed and soon the local police officer's car turned off the main road towards our place.

May walked out to greet the officer as he donned his cap instead of removing it as he usually did when just paying a friendly visit. Slightly embarrassed, the policeman said, 'Hello, Mrs Hunt, how are you today? The usual good mood, I hope?'

'Of course I'm in a good mood. Why? What's this all about?'

'Seems you had a bit of a run-in with our postmaster the other day.'

'Yes, we did have a bit of a run-in, if that's what you'd call it. Nothing terribly wrong happened. I think we ended up about even.'

'Well, Mrs Hunt, I'm afraid the postmaster doesn't see it that way. He has issued this summons. You are being charged with assault and are required to attend the courthouse here at nine in the morning on the day stated on the summons.'

May raised her eyebrows.

'Mr Henderson, the manager of Urisino Station, is a justice of the peace so he will hear the matter. I think you know him.'

May nodded.

As word of the summons spread, what had been considered to be a fading piece of gossip took on a new momentum. On the decreed day of the hearing, May walked the mile to town. She entered the police station's front gate, walked onto the verandah and knocked.

Senior Constable Tarrant called May in and walked with her through the hallway and into the courtroom, where she was asked to sit in the dock. She awaited the proceedings feeling extremely isolated.

The courtroom was large and forbidding with highly polished brown benches and railings separating the gallery from the seating area provided for juries. A little further on was another bench that was enclosed by a guard-rail with a small gate. This was normally occupied by the accused. Directly opposite was the witness stand, which was close to the raised bench to be occupied by the judge, but in this case a justice of the peace.

This poorly lit room, tucked in the bowels of the old weatherboard police station, had nothing to suggest that it had any connection with the outside world. The other occupants of the room were the complainant, an agitated, fidgety little man, and a local grazier, who was an amused uncle of the complainant. He lounged casually on a cedar bench in the gallery. He had tried unsuccessfully to talk his nephew into dropping the charges and avoid embarrassment. Sitting further along was the stoutly built, grey-haired Frank Kennedy, who was the not-too-popular hotel-keeper. He had just come for a look.

The man in charge of the proceedings was the manager of one of the biggest grazing properties in New South Wales, Mr Henderson. He was a conservative man and noted for his limited dialogue with people of any standing. He displayed agitation that suggested he found the predicament to be distasteful. Proceedings got under way. The oath was dispensed with and the charge of assault was read out. May pleaded 'guilty'.

Taking into consideration the evidence and guilty plea, the only thing that remained was for justice to take its course. In accordance with the law, a sentence of '£2 or four days imprisonment' was pronounced. There was silence.

After what seemed an eternity, May spoke. 'I have no money to pay the fine so I will just have to go to gaol. I suppose you men will take good care of my goats, fowls and garden as well as my five children.' Not so much a question as a statement, May stared hard at the men in the room. While the case brought before the court had been dealt with, the real issue was unfolding.

There was quiet turmoil in the courtroom and May displayed a calm dignity. After surveying the situation she spoke again and her words brought some relief.

'Seeing that nothing is going to happen here, I might as well go home.' With composure she stood with great dignity, then walked from the court. Frank Kennedy, the publican, followed May out and insisted that she accept the £2 he offered for the fine.

'Mr Kennedy, I haven't got any money and I don't know when I can pay you back.'

'Mrs Hunt, I don't want repayment. This is a sign of respect for a rare act of courage and common sense. Please take it.'

There was another occasion when the same businessman refused to release cash-on-delivery parcels of clothing from the post office because our store's food account was overdue. As the parcels had not been collected by the due date they were returned to the supplier. May wrote and explained why the goods were not collected and they were again posted to Wanaaring and released on demand.

Yet another problem surfaced when he supplied a substitute mixture of his own for baking powder. May refused to accept the alternative, stating that he was being paid by the government to supply real baking powder and it should only be real baking powder she received. He argued that May had to take what he was offering.

In response, she threw the pseudo baking powder at his head. It missed its target and burst against the shelves. Undaunted, May calmly walked behind the counter and helped herself to the equivalent amount of real baking powder. Shortly after she left, May looked back and saw Senior Constable Tarrant walking across to the store. There was never any action taken, nor was there any more substitution of foodstuffs.

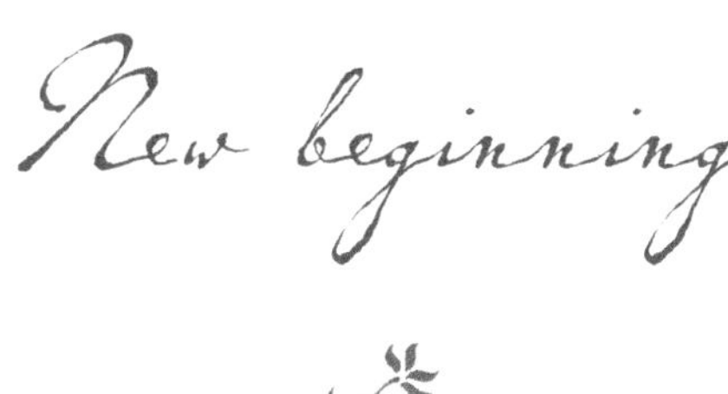

The years rolled on. We grew older and as eleven, twelve and thirteen year olds we took time out from school to do a few days work. We helped with lamb-marking and worked at shearing time, or would spend a few days with a drover until he was able to replace us with an adult.

With May working so hard, we all wanted to get out and start putting money back into the home to make her life easier. As well as making most of the girls' clothes, she kept patching and mending, which was an endless job. She was fussy about us being clean and tidy, even in our knockabout clothes. Life was hard but she never complained and didn't seem to tire. Occasionally we would hear her quietly sobbing during the night.

When all the chores were done, there was time to relax with music or needlework. May was in her forties and those hands which pulled and threaded wire on fencing jobs with her husband in her twenties and continued to cut and load wood during her thirties were now producing some of the finest embroidery imaginable. May manoeuvred fine needles and coloured cotton

Piece of May's embroidery that got a blue ribbon at Broken Hill's Silver City annual show.

into beautiful designs on tablecloths, pillowslips and cushion covers, and on clothes for her and the girls. The work was good enough to take out a blue ribbon at Broken Hill's annual Silver City show. May's needlework was in demand among many of the Wanaaring locals as well as from passers-by.

Eventually the big day came when I was able to leave school and get a job on Ularara Station, seven miles from home and the place where May used to do her ten bob a week laundry job. I was working around the house as a kind of general hand doing very little of the stock work that I always wanted to do.

That job was my introduction to how white people lived when no one was watching them. I discovered they were not all that different to us and they didn't seem to be all that fussy about anything more than May was. They were good people but when any of their friends came for a meal I had to sit in the kitchen, even though I used to dress up in my good clothes for tea every night.

A few months later another station job was offered. It was on Barona Station, a little further from home but I was able to get back most weekends. I was on a horse at least once a week and sometimes daily for weeks at a time, especially preparing for shearing or when the water was drying up in mid-summer.

I was content in that job. I got on well with the owner, Charley Gibbons and his wife, and I was made to feel at home. I dined with them, no matter who was there. I used to stay up in the main house and listen to the radio. It was the early stages of World War Two, so apart from the war news, there were community concerts broadcast across the country. One day Mrs Gibbons asked quietly, 'Harold, do you think you and I could manage the place should Charley go to war?'

'Of course we could,' was my firm reply.

I learned so much working for Charley and his brother Jack, who was now the owner of Wanaaring Station. The older brother, Nelson, owned and resided at Mulgany Bore, eighteen miles west of Wanaaring. The three brothers worked together a good bit of the time. They were all interested in machinery and windmills and were forever trying new ways of doing things. That gave me the opportunity to learn about bush work as well as general station work. The work was never boring and I learnt new things all the time. It was only occasionally that I'd not go home at weekends and it was on one of these times my employers returned with news for me.

'Harold, when we go into Wanaaring next weekend you must come. May has a big surprise for you. She said you will never guess.'

There was a big week of wondering. A gramophone? A horse? The day arrived and we crossed the Paroo next to our place and a tall pole standing beside the bough shed caught my eye. This sight told me nothing until I hurried into the bough shed. There it was. A wireless! The only ones I had ever seen were table models. But this was a three-foot-high Stromberg Carlson powered by a

ABOVE *Friends Paddy Johnston, Jimmy Gaulton, Mum, Doreen, Beulah, Eric, cousin Ron Riley in font.*
BELOW *Hunt family – Rachel, Beulah, Doreen, Roy, Harold, Eric, cousin Keith Quayle and Janet the dog.*
The occasion was the visit to Wanaaring by Governor Lord and Lady Wakehurst.

Swimming spot at Hunt's place on Paroo River at Wanaaring.
Uncle Harry Knight, Roy Hunt, Rupert Crowe and Gilbert Bates –
the diver must be Superman.

six-volt car battery. We had two batteries, which were alternated because it was necessary to send them to Bourke to be recharged.

To many people, it would not have meant very much. But to someone who grew up understanding that there was a big difference between wants and needs, I was overwhelmed that May would spend her hard-earned money on what I considered to be a luxury.

Before the arrival of our wireless we would play the gramophone. It was a matter of listening closely and hurrying to lift the speaker as soon as the record had reached the end of the playing section. There wasn't an automatic lift and return on those old wind-up machines. Another problem was that we would often overwind them and break the main spring. May became an expert at mending gramophone springs. She would heat the broken parts, punch holes in each piece and insert a copper rivet, the same type that she used to mend leather harnesses. That was effective until after a few mends the spring became too short and would only play half the record, so it meant a letter off to Mark Gilbert's music stores in Sydney for another spring for the gramophone.

With the arrival of the wireless we could listen to such programs as 'Dad and Dave', 'Mrs Hobbs', 'Martin's Corner' and the like. There was also the overseas news, which was always about the war, although as a youth I did not feel that this was very important. It belonged to another world.

New relationship

So many things happened over the fourteen-year period we lived at Wanaaring. With all of that, May never wavered from her goal of raising her family. She was still an attractive woman and no doubt enchanted many of the men who came her way. But May had a family to raise. Only when she had achieved and consolidated what she felt was her work did she begin to give some thought to herself. She eventually accepted a man into her life.

May entered into an intermittent relationship with a fellow called Jim Hennessey. Jim worked for and resided with his brother Tom, the owner of Backward Station, some thirty miles up the river from Wanaaring. The brothers were not involved in any kind of social or sporting activities other than the annual race meetings at the local townships of Wanaaring and Hungerford. Tom regularly consumed alcohol and as such decided that, although he owned a reliable motor vehicle, he would never learn to drive. That would be the job for Jim or anyone else working on the property. So when Tom needed to have one of his frequent benders on the booze, someone would have to drive him to Wanaaring. His drinking

LEFT *May and Coral with family dog Janet in the garden at Wanaaring.*

RIGHT *Mum, Coral and Ethel Riley at Wanaaring.*

binges would last days. Jim, being a teetotaller, spent his time sitting on the hotel verandah chatting to anyone who came by.

Jim's other job was to replenish the grocery supplies, which included fresh vegetables from our garden. These visits to buy the vegetables were the beginnings of a relationship that lasted many years. May and Jim never lived together as husband and wife, even though two children were born. Cyril and Coral were both registered in the name of Hennessey.

Despite having her hands full raising her family, May always took on extra work that would bring in a little more money.

Men working on surrounding stations used to send their blue serge suits and white silk shirts in by mail for May to clean and press, to be worn at the monthly dances. I remember May heating the flat irons on a sheet of tin over the open fire, then rubbing them on the bare earth and on a piece of rough bag material and finally on a clean piece of linen. She would iron over a dampened piece of linen to get the steam-pressed effect required to make the garment hold its crease.

The Wanaaring hotel offered May the laundry work when Myrtle became ill. Then the Robinsons of Ularara Station offered their washing and ironing to be done at their home seven miles from Wanaaring. The grazier, Tom Robinson, would transport May to and from their place and she would get her midday meal with morning and afternoon teas and ten shillings for doing the weekly laundry of up to six adults.

One day while doing the hotel's laundry, May was lifting a

bucket of water from an underground tank, as there was no tap in the laundry. The extra weight caused her to break a bone in her foot. It was some time before May was able to attract the attention of the hotel people, as the laundry was some fifty yards away. Eventually her calls were heard and the bush nurse came and examined the swollen foot. The nurse strapped it and instructed May to keep off it. There was no thought of an x-ray or further checking and no consideration as to how she would manage to care for her children.

The hotel owner eventually transported May home but that was the last she heard from him. Due to the extreme swelling she had to remove the bandage and bathe her foot in as hot a bath as she could stand, several times a day, and stay in bed with her foot in a raised position.

The only children at home were the school-aged children who would provide May and themselves with breakfast, pack school lunches for themselves, see to the fowls and goats, water the garden and then go off to school. In the afternoon, they would complete their other chores and with instructions from May, an evening meal would be prepared and served. It was hard going.

The situation lasted several days until rescue arrived in the shape of a police detective by the name of Jack Deakin and his tracker, Frank Williams. Their disgust at May's predicament brought immediate action. The publican at the Wanaaring hotel was ordered to pay at least one visit per day to check on May and provide meals for her and the children. With further advice from the police, there also eventuated some financial compensation.

Changes

Things began to change. No doubt May could see the inevitable. As we grew older there was no permanent employment other than the isolation of working on outback station properties. There was no chance that we would marry into the local community because we were Aboriginal and other Aboriginal families never stayed around long enough to form any kind of lasting relationship. The family at home dwindled.

Our horizons widened and we met people from other towns. Us boys working with drovers would get the opportunity to visit places such as Bourke. There were picture shows and shops with their tempting variety of clothes as well as machinery and grocery stores the likes of which we had never seen before. And there was a train station that opened the door to the rest of the world.

My eldest sister, Doreen, now aged seventeen, got a job at Yancannia, one of the big stations which was closer to White Cliffs than to Wanaaring. There was not even the possibility of weekend visits nor were there any phone calls as we didn't have a phone. Doreen used to write regularly but the weekly mail service to Yancannia did not always connect with the service from Wilcannia to Wanaaring. Some of Doreen's letters would take up to two weeks to get to their destination. Our younger sister Rachel was still at school and spent time with Doreen during the holidays.

After a few months at Yancannia, Doreen moved to Wongalilly, a smaller property nearer home. The Billings owned this property and Doreen was able to go into Wilcannia every few weeks. It enabled her to shop, post letters or send a telegram saying she was well and happy. The Billings no longer had any children at home so they treated Doreen like a daughter.

Beulah, on leaving school at fifteen, began work as a domestic at the hotel in Hungerford, and a local gossipmonger spread a yarn that Beulah was pregnant. That was a huge blow. May was beginning to enjoy her well-brought-up children becoming respectable adults.

May called the proprietor of the Hungerford hotel and told him that Beulah was to return home on the next mail truck. The hotelier was aghast when told why. He assured May that there was no truth in that rumour at all. Beulah was considered part of the hotelier's family. She was highly respected for her work ethic as well as for her moral standards. The hotelier tried to calm May but she was adamant that Beulah should return home. May then thanked him for his kindness, generosity and support.

Doreen, Mum with Cyril, Harold and Roy.

Due to the rumours, Beulah had to give up her job at great emotional and financial cost. May took her to Bourke for a thorough medical check-up, which confirmed Beulah's story. Nothing else could be done other than to keep the rumour mongers waiting for an event that was never going to happen.

Moving on

May did not cry often but I do remember her grief when she lost her father, and then later had to come to terms with the loss of her niece Hannah Riley, and of course dear Teddy and Myrtle. They were sad and lonely times for her.

May was upset, too, when I arrived home and declared that I had left the station job on Barona after having worked there for more than a year. At this job, I was considered reliable, even at an early age, to be responsible for the day-to-day duties of the place. I had been left in charge of the entire property while Charley and his wife spent two weeks holidaying in Brisbane.

Another time was when our sheep were being trucked away. May had heard from some of the local graziers that the Bourke abattoir was sending stock transport around the district buying up sheep. They were looking to make up a full load. May knew that she would have to let the sheep go as it was nearing the end of her family's stay at Wanaaring. She took the opportunity to make a sale. When the truck arrived, we already had the goats and sheep yarded. As they were being drafted May turned away and I could see that she was crying.

I got a lump in my throat and only then was I able to understand the situation. May was seeing another part of her life draw to a close. She had put her soul into Wanaaring and had raised her family there. It was surrounded by extraordinary memories.

Christmas was the ultimate. No matter how long we were away, it was important to be home for Christmas. Us boys would cut and cart extra bows to cover the weather-worn holes in the old shed. The girls would help May with the food and hang up streamers and balloons and set the big old wooden stools at the table.

The smaller children would be seated along one side of the table and the other sides would be cramped with as many four-gallon drums as possible. This was to seat whoever might happen to arrive on the day. If travellers were passing by, they would be offered a four-gallon drum at the big old table. If someone camped alone by the river, they would be asked to join us. No matter how many invited guests were in attendance, there was always that emotional emptiness if there was a missing family member.

I was eighteen when I spent my first Christmas away from home. With well-made plans in order, I'd been working on a station further west of Wanaaring, breaking in horses and doing general station work. This meant there would be a reasonable amount of money for May to buy any extras she might need. Instead of going directly home at the year's end, I somehow managed to finish work near Wilcannia. There were a few shops there – shops where I could buy presents for the family and so the spree was on. A week's wages went on presents and on things not available in the little general store back home.

By the time I'd satisfied my buying urge, I was broke. I could not even afford my fare home. There would not have been a problem getting a free ride home with the mailman as I could always pay the fare later. But my pride got in the way. Since getting out and earning a living, May's teachings were continually coming up. I had developed a strong sense of commitment and having to pay my own way.

It was only a few days before Christmas and I was able to get a job on Menamurtee Station, some twenty miles west of Wilcannia. There was no telephone to our place in those days so I had to send a telegram. What a blow that would have been. The message was clear – another unoccupied oil drum at the Christmas table.

That Christmas was different to any I'd had before. No Santa, no presents and no one for me to give the presents to. However, I did receive one present and that was two bottles of beer. The station manager gave all hands two bottles of beer. To me, that signified that I was a grown man at last.

I had tried to act the role of the family man when I was growing up but now I was accepted as one. Two bottles of beer was all that was necessary for me to get merry and I was able to do that without fear of anyone looking critically at me. I was one of the boys. To be a little boozed at Christmas, I thought, was the way to go. Spending the most important time of the year away from home made it easier for me to move on.

Move to Bourke

After I left Barona Station, Jack Gibbons told me about a drover who was taking delivery of a mob of sheep from his property at Wanaaring. He was looking for a horse-tailer. They were going to Bourke, which was a journey of three weeks. I got the job but, after one of the many disputes I had with the boss, I only stayed two weeks and returned home.

Jack Rushton, another drover from Yantabulla, employed me and that job lasted two months. Smaller jobs came my way until eventually I was employed by the Water Conservation and Irrigation Commission on an artesian drilling plant, which meant only getting home a couple of times a year. It did pay a reasonable and regular wage, which meant some financial security for May.

I moved on and spent some time on the railways in Broken Hill, then did some truck driving for John Boland of the White Cliffs store. It was inevitable that I would eventually enter the shearing industry, which meant being away for longer and longer periods. Though May was still an emotional and spiritual anchor, Wanaaring, to me, no longer felt like my home.

Mum with her two youngest children, Cyril and Coral.

By the time Cyril was nine and Coral three, the rest of us had left Wanaaring. In my youthfulness, all that I could see was what I wanted for me and I continually thought that May could simply pack up and move to Bourke. It was while away on one of these extended lapses from home that I received word she had done exactly that.

May understood that what was happening was another stage in her life. Doreen, Beulah and Rachel were now all in Bourke. Doreen had her cooking job at the Durham private hospital. The other two would no doubt get a job. Roy was married and moving around the country doing contract fencing. Eric and I were shearing. Letters became the fragile link that kept us together. The letters we sent to May sometimes had a cheque enclosed and usually no return address.

Wanaaring was no longer our home. It used to be the centre for so many travellers, black and white, rich and poor, the elderly and the young. There was spirit in that piece of land. It became a piece of dusty earth upon which I sat and cried when I returned many years later.

May slowly wound up her home. She arranged for a place to leave the horses and she knew that the goats would care for themselves. The sheep had already been sold, as had the fowls.

The furniture was not a problem as it was made from round bush timber and packing cases. There were cooking utensils, big old iron saucepans and camp ovens, some too cumbersome to be packed so they were left to be brought later, along with the wagonette. However, the wireless, gramophone and dozens of records had to be packed carefully for the long journey on the back of the mail truck over corrugated miles of dirt road to Bourke.

New life

May had hardly ever been to Bourke and on each occasion it was to have a baby. All she remembered was the hospital and the long, hot dusty journey. She was now entering a new era in her life. Only many years later did May mention her sadness at leaving Wanaaring.

Her new home was a single room at the North Bourke hotel, four miles from Bourke. Somehow she had found herself a job and it provided board and lodgings for herself and the two children, along with a small wage in return for cooking for the owner, Frederick Warmoll, his daughters Muffy and Googie, and a yardman.

This job was merely a means of passing the time. May was well-liked and respected by those with whom she was living. Cyril and Coral were happy and they were able to see their older sisters fairly regularly.

The stay at North Bourke was therefore no more than a resting period and for May to have the opportunity to find a permanent home. After several months in that job an opportunity did arise. It came in the form of an old unlicensed pub, the former Club House Hotel. The building was in good order but the licence had been transferred to another town. May saw this as not only a place for herself and her immediate family, but an opportunity to provide food and shelter for others.

One issue, however, could not be overlooked. May was Aboriginal and therefore not an Australian citizen. Such a public facility or business could not be registered to her. Seeing the need for accommodation in the town, May thought there was some way around the situation. There was. She was prepared to apply for an Exemption Certificate, which would remove her from any entitlements of the NSW Aborigines Protection Act. It was a temporary release from the restrictions of the Act and would help her carry out what she had in mind.

The Aborigines Board soon approached May. The details of the exemption were spelt out and, while she felt contempt for the agreement, she conceded. It appeared to be the only way for her to achieve her goal. The procedure to obtain this Exemption Certificate meant that May had to get character references from two local businesspeople – a justice of the peace and a senior police officer. None of that proved to be a problem. So after a visit to the local courthouse to get the paperwork sorted out, May's family-style boarding house was born.

May was more of a mother than a landlady to those who availed themselves of her hospitality. There were family units adjacent to the main building so there were many children. There was the business side to deal with as well as the monthly trading accounts. The business houses in town accepted May's patronage. The butcher and baker were both happy to conduct business with her.

It was a well-run boarding house that catered for full-time resident families and the travelling public. Drovers working from Bourke would leave their families there, enabling the children to attend school. Married shearers from other parts of the country were able to have their families in the safety and comfort at May's while they worked the shearing season in the district.

Often on Saturday nights, the dining room tables and chairs would be pushed against the walls and old-time dancing would go on into the late hours. May with her accordion supplied the music. There was one very strict rule. No alcohol. If any person arrived back on the premises intoxicated, they were instructed to go to their room and stay there or to pack their bags and leave. People usually respected the rule.

Some boarders availed themselves of the meals and the comfort of their rooms, and went about their lives uninvolved with the staff or other boarders. Others took the opportunity to enjoy a surrogate family. Then there were those who saw an opportunity to get free board and lodgings. They would arrive with a tale of woe, explaining their money would be coming in the

.W.B. 19.

NEW SOUTH W[illegible] GOVERNMENT
ABORIGINES PROTECTION [illegible]CT, 1909-1943, SECTION 18c
[REGU[illegible]ION 56.]

CERTIFICATE [illegible]F EXEMPTION

From Provisions of [illegible] Act and Regulations

THIS IS TO CERTIFY that [illegible]
[illegible] Aborigine, aged 20 years, re[illegible]ing at Hope Street, [illegible]
person who in the opinion of the Aborigi[illegible]s Welfare Board, ought no longer be [illegible]
provisions
following provisions of the Aborigines [illegible]otection Act and Regulations, or any o[illegible]
[illegible]ions, and he/she is accordingly exempted from such provisions:—

[illegible] in compliance with the Resolution of the
[illegible]rigines Welfare Board and dated the [illegible]
day of January 1953

[illegible]hairman.
of the Aborigines Welfare Board. [illegible]lember.
[illegible]ountersigned by
[illegible]he Secretary.

ABOVE *May Hunt's Exemption Certificate.*
The certificates were referred to by Aboriginal people as 'dog tags'.
BELOW *May Hunt with daughters Doreen and Rachel.*

May and friend at boarding house in Bourke, 1950.

next mail and in the morning that person's chair at the breakfast table would be vacant.

It wasn't long before Rachel and Eric were able to travel back to Wanaaring to pack up May's house. Once there, they set about greasing the axles of the wagonette, and checked loose nuts and couplings in preparation for the long journey back to Bourke. The horses were no trouble to find as they had been left to graze in the Wanaaring Station paddock. Sorting through the remnants of fourteen years of growing up was hard for Rachel and Eric. There were memories everywhere.

A growing family

While May prepared breakfasts and got on with her life, her family was still expanding. Doreen met and married Eddie Suckling, a young happy-go-lucky, hard-working former miner from Broken Hill. Beulah married Bert Parlett from Mudgee. Bert was in great demand by truck owners in the mail and general transport business in and around Bourke. Bert, his mother and a couple of his younger brothers made the Club House boarding house their permanent home until it was eventually vacated.

Eric's partner, Jo, and my own, Nellie, were on the staff at the boarding house. Both women had been married before. Jo had two young sons from her previous marriage, and Nellie was the mother of one-year-old John. The two women soon became members of the Hunt clan and May became a grandmother and achieved another milestone.

In 1950, May became a justice of the peace. She was often engaged by the local police to accompany them when escorting women who had been sentenced at Bourke court to be imprisoned at Bathurst or Sydney.

May soon purchased an old 1927 Whippet car and did some unlicensed driving around Bourke. This inspired her to do some independent travelling. On one adventure while travelling with Cyril and Coral, May noticed the rear wheel falling apart. She was on her way to visit her mother, Hannah Quayle, in Wilcannia. The problem was noticed not far from Bourke, close to where there was a caretaker of a public government watering place. The fellow happened to be a handy sort of bloke and was able to repair the wheel.

One day while in Wilcannia, there came a message for May from the local police sergeant who wished to see her. Not one to put things off, she contacted the sergeant, who very apologetically asked if she would kindly go to the hospital and transport a patient to her home in the Malley, an Aboriginal suburb of Wilcannia. There was no mention of licence or registration.

May made the best of the few days in Wilcannia. She enjoyed reminiscing with her mother and other family and friends. Her confidence with the car increased as she practised driving around the town. May soon developed enough confidence to take on the dusty outback roads and visit some of her old stomping grounds.

She eventually headed west to White Cliffs, sixty miles away. During a short stopover she showed Cyril and Coral where we had camped many years before and visited the cemetery where Jack Quayle, Teddy and other close relatives were interred. She also looked at some of the old opal diggings before going on to the station where Laurie was working. On the way they passed Morden, where her family life had all begun.

They travelled on and spent a few days in the company of Laurie and his family. It gave May the opportunity to enjoy camp life again. She went hunting with her brother as they had done some twenty-five years before.

After an enjoyable week, it was time to move on to Wanaaring to see Jack Gibbons and his family. May stopped there for a short visit. These people were the last of her era who were still in close proximity. May's journey was about grieving and saying goodbye, and it was a matter of putting the past behind her as well as strengthening the bonds she had with the land on which so much of her life was spent. A drive of 118 miles on a graded road back to Bourke was an easy and comfortable affair, after having traversed some of the roughest roads in the Corner Country.

Not long after May and the little ones returned, there came a notice from Bun Tancred, head of the Bourke abattoir, saying that their property, the former Club House Hotel presently occupied by May, had to be vacated. That was the beginning of several court battles with the owners, Tancred Brothers Pty Ltd, one of the country's biggest meat-producing companies. They wanted to demolish the building by a certain date but that date did not suit May.

May used every delaying tactic available to continue to provide a roof over the heads of her family and friends until she was satisfied that all would be well. She was unhappy with the way Bun

ABOVE *Granny Quayle.*

BELOW *May and some relations during the White Cliffs tour to visit family in her unregistered Whippet car.*

ABOVE *May with ten grandchildren of the Parlett family, Beulah's mob.*

BELOW *Coral and Cyril in front of Mum's car.*

Tancred was going about removing her. One of his tactics was to arrive in the early mornings, unannounced. Accompanied by people he never bothered to introduce, he would issue ultimatums.

Eventually an eviction order was served. May engaged a solicitor who agreed to represent her and help delay the closure of the boarding house to a date more suitable to those presently housed there. On the day of the court hearing, there was an extremely late message from her solicitor to say he was unable to attend or to even advise May as to any alternative. The situation appeared grim until another local woman let it be known that her solicitor, Frank Davidson from Wellington, might help. Frank was well-known and was recognised for his assistance to the poor. In no time at all, he had the matter dismissed. Frank had pointed out that the eviction notice was invalid because the server of the notice, Bun Tancred, was unauthorised to act in that capacity. It was a small win.

In the meantime, a cottage was being built for May in another part of town. It was only half completed when she finally said, 'Alright, all my staff and boarders are satisfactorily situated now. I'll go.'

A private life

After some time May purchased a caravan and used to get people such as family, friends and mail contractors to move her to whatever place she wished to spend time at. On one of these journeys, May decided to spend time in Wilcannia with her ageing mother, Hannah. One day, Hannah called her only surviving offspring, May and Sonny, into her home and asked them to sit down and listen carefully.

'May and Sonny, I want to tell you something,' she said in her Malyangapa language. 'Now don't start getting upset 'cos I got something important to tell you. I gotta tell you two now. I don't want no crying and all that, 'cos everything is gonna be alright. I'm going to join your father. I'm going to be with him soon and all those others that went that way, too. They'll all be there.'

Of course May and Sonny broke down. To hear their mother talk so calmly about her own passing was very emotional. Hannah Quayle showed a great deal of concern for those she was leaving behind but she was ready for her journey. A few days later she had a mild stroke and was admitted to hospital. Shortly afterwards,

May contracted a virus and was also admitted. This meant she was next to her mother when she died.

Despite the rustling of leaves on the giant gums, the bird calls and the clear blue sky, there was a dark cloud over Wilcannia on the day of Hannah Quayle's funeral. Every household was getting out its Sunday best. The town was getting dressed up to say farewell to 'Granny Hannah Quayle'. Granny Hannah had been seen every pension day in the main street sitting on the bench near the post office or on a seat in Wilcannia's biggest store, Knox & Downs. Today they were all going to say farewell.

By the time the cortege arrived at the cemetery gates, the grounds were full with people. To have the whole district share in the family's sorrow was not unexpected.

May's life had entered yet another stage. Her father had lived into his sixties but three of her sisters and her youngest brother died before reaching forty. Her youngest sister was only forty-two when she was taken with cancer. May took her grieving to as much family as possible and always appeared to recover with more strength.

Slowing down

May now felt the need to settle somewhere closer to the main bulk of her family.

Malyangapa country was a long way away. Having a good knowledge of the whole of New South Wales and Queensland, May decided that she would settle in Wellington, New South Wales.

She found herself a cottage in a short street with no through traffic, friendly neighbours and just a block from the main shopping area. There were several other aged pensioners as well as families with primary-school-aged children. The railway station was also close by. Her backyard was large enough for her caravan to be parked. The caravan was kept in case her wanderlust got the better of her. It also served as extra accommodation when family or friends were visiting.

May was always immaculately dressed. She would often be seen chatting over the fence to a neighbour or on her front verandah mending a broken chair or another piece of furniture. The neighbours' children called often to see if they could run errands for her and to listen to the stories of where she grew up.

She told them traditional stories just as they had been told to her sixty-odd years before.

Wellington was close to most major sporting events and May loved sport. She was fond of horse racing but also loved seeing people competing and enjoying themselves, particularly children. All her children were athletic but it was Cyril, the youngest, who excelled. He played football and tennis and showed talent in boxing. However, his true success came in cycling until a couple of accidents, an enlarged heart and some exuberant living shortened his time in the sport.

Before May's enthusiasm for cycling lessened, another cyclist arrived on the scene. Her grandson Michael joined the high rollers of the velodromes around Australia. May was rejuvenated. It seemed that she was determined to see some of her offspring make it big in some sport. Michael, Rachel's only child, took over where Cyril had left off. It was not long before Michael was noticed and groomed by the local cycling experts in Dubbo and Wellington. May knew that he would make it to the top.

Michael matched the best in the Western area and then rode in Sydney. Before long he was in the hands of Olympic cycling coach Alex Fulcher, and made the semi-finals of the 1956 Melbourne Olympics.

A knock on May's door one morning by Rachel stirred her from slumber. 'Come on! We're headed for Sydney. Michael is riding in the Australian championships tonight at Wiley Park.'

That night, Michael added two Australian titles to his belt and came second in a third event. He had achieved the ultimate for his most devoted supporter.

There were times when I arrived at May's place to the strains of music, a schottische or an old-time waltz being played on her button accordion.

May showed signs that she was beginning to slow down. Her face looked tired and her body was weary. We all noticed these changes, however May thought otherwise. Her only health problems were some weight gain and high blood pressure. Even on her bad days, May's spirits were high, and she would speak of her discomfort then move on. She had no trouble talking about her illness but she never dwelled on it. When the end was near there were signs that she knew.

My family and I were living in Sydney at the time and, instead of returning to her cottage in Wellington, May decided to spend some time with us. Her stay was calm and peaceful and we reminisced about life. We talked about many things and left nothing unsaid. May and my wife Nell were very close and on this occasion May told Nell that she was moving on, that she had heard from her deceased relations and it was her time to go.

Mum at her van in Wilcannia visiting her mother in 1964.

May then stayed with Cyril and his family before spending time with Coral, who was nearby. It was during her stay with her youngest that May eventually passed over. After lunch one day she quietly told Coral that she was tired and needed an afternoon rest, and so it was on 25 February 1974 that May passed away.

While I knew May was not going to live forever, I don't ever recall thinking about her passing on, and today I still feel her comforting presence and laughter.

She was a person who could express anger or happiness according to the situation at hand. She was incapable of hatred, and discouraged it in all who came her way. To meet her was a comfort within itself. Her quiet, confident ways made every new acquaintance feel like a friend of old. Her soft, gentle manner portrayed strength and dignity, a characteristic carried with great pride by her family as we moved through adolescence to adulthood.

After almost seventy-four years of hardship, trauma and sadness, mixed with large doses of joy and happiness, Mother departed this life peacefully to rest among the spirits who guided her.

May Hunt, her abiding love and wisdom, like the sun, the wind, the earth and the open spaces she loved, are not gone but are woven into the fabric of this age-old land of her ancestors.

I could write so much more but I believe I can hear her saying, 'That's enough, thank you son. You were always one who never knew when to stop.'

God has her in His keeping, we have her in our hearts.

Mother

There are always tales of mothers, tales of love to tell
How they nurture us through childhood, how they comfort us so well.

From the time of our conception, to the days when we are old
A mother's love is with us, as our lives unfold.

As happy little children, beside our mother's knee
We are taught the principles of life, how to walk, to talk, to see.

Whilst some of us might stumble and often lose the way
The thought is always with us, 'What would my mother say?'

Despite the tears I'd caused her with the selfish life I'd run
Her arms would fold around me, 'Come sit with me dear son.'

The day the angels called her, Mum was well aware
She said goodbye to all the family, in her youngest daughter's care.

I know you've settled in dear Mum, in the big camp up above
And you've bound your offspring all as one, with your everlasting love.

Departed brothers

To the memory of Ted and Bill

Ted and Bill you left us, you moved on through the day
You paved the way to heaven boys, paid the price we all must pay
You gave us joy and happiness, you left memories that will last
Your spirit is forever with us, though many years have passed.

Dear Father went to join you and May did as well
They stayed to build the family and now with you they dwell
It's always sad when loved ones leave: they answer to God's call
We grieve the loss of those we love; it is no loss at all.

You were chosen from God's garden, to prepare a place above
And boys before you left us, you gave us so much love
We will one day be with you, your siblings, Mum and Dad
And as each one departs this life, that parting will be sad.

I know that while you're waiting, you must smile now and then
At us earthly mortals, who know not where and when
I know you're watching over us, to guide us through each day
God chose you to lead us, he chose you to show the way.

There are many people who helped me to keep going with this book.
To you all I say a sincere and humble thank you.
Special thanks to writer Anne Beveridge.
For what she taught me I will be forever grateful.

Harold Hunt

ABOUT THE AUTHOR

Harold Hunt is well-known in New South Wales for his work in cross-cultural communication and Indigenous health. He has spent many years working as an educator and counsellor in the area of substance abuse and most recently has been a lecturer at Charles Sturt University in Dubbo, NSW. His novel *Gorn Shearin* was published in 2002. He published his autobiography *Along My Way* in 2016.

This is a Magabala Book
LEADING PUBLISHER OF ABORIGINAL AND
TORRES STRAIT ISLANDER STORYTELLERS.
CHANGING THE WORLD, ONE STORY AT A TIME.

First published 2006, new revised edition published 2022
Magabala Books Aboriginal Corporation
1 Bagot Street, Broome, Western Australia
Website: www.magabala.com
Email: sales@magabala.com

Magabala Books receives financial assistance from the Commonwealth Government through the Australia Council, its arts advisory body. The State of Western Australia has made an investment in this project through the Department of Local Government, Sport and Cultural Industries. Magabala Books would like to acknowledge the generous support of the Shire of Broome, Western Australia.

Magabala Books is Australia's only independent Aboriginal and Torres Strait Islander publishing house. Magabala Books acknowledges the Traditional Owners of the Country on which we live and work. We recognise the unbroken connection to traditional lands, waters and cultures. Through what we publish, we honour all our Elders, peoples and stories, past, present and future.

Cover Design Jo Hunt
Cover image David Foster / Alamy Stock Photo
Typeset by Post Pre-press Group
Printed and bound by Griffin Press, South Australia

ISBN 978-1-922613-83-7 (Print)
ISBN 978-1-922613-79-0 (ePUB)
ISBN 978-1-922613-80-6 (ePDF)